Sociocide

Sociocide

Reflections on Today's Wars

Keith Doubt

LEXINGTON BOOKS
Lanham • Boulder • New York • London

Published by Lexington Books
An imprint of The Rowman & Littlefield Publishing Group, Inc.
4501 Forbes Boulevard, Suite 200, Lanham, Maryland 20706
www.rowman.com

6 Tinworth Street, London SE11 5AL, United Kingdom

British Library Cataloguing in Publication Information Available

Library of Congress Cataloging-in-Publication Data

ISBN 9781793623843 (cloth)
ISBN 9781793623867 (pbk)
ISBN 9781793623850 (electronic)

To Victor Ayoub, in memoriam

Contents

Preface

There are a number of astute, analytical studies of modern wars and their political and social consequences. One thing the studies address is the agency of the US government in initiating reckless and thoughtless wars in Afghanistan, Iraq, and Syria. Some are written by journalists. Some by historians. Some by political scientists.

This book, *Sociocide: Reflections on Today's Wars,* learns from and draws upon these works. I, though, need to identify what is particular about the study. *Sociocide: Reflections on Today's Wars* is a sociological study drawing also upon anthropology, philosophy, and literature. The approach the book takes is theoretical, formulating, developing, and applying the notion of sociocide, a neologism, meaning to kill society. Sociocide is developed as a Weberian ideal type. The purpose is to provide meaningfully adequate accounts of the human, social, and political consequences of today's wars. The focus is somewhat different from comparable books in journalism, history, and political science; the focus is to develop a conceptual account of today's wars, one that is objective and moral, critical and humanistic.

The study has benefited from the discussions that took place with students at Wittenberg University in the seminar, "War, Identity, and Justice" and from the editorial assistance of Peggy Hanna and Sophia Reutter.

Chapter One

On Sociocide

What is sociocide? We know other "-cide" words: suicide, homocide, fratricide, regicide, urbicide, and, the most frightening, genocide. Sociocide is not found in the dictionary. It is a neologism. It means to kill society. Sociocide is the murdering of the social encompassing matters pertaining to human solidarity: family, social institutions, gender, ethnic, racial, and national identity.

It is possible to kill a city or nearly kill a city. Consider the tragedies of Aleppo in Syria, Sarajevo in Bosnia-Herzegovina, Vukovar in former-Yugoslavia, Leningrad in Russia, Nagasaki in Japan, and Dresden in Germany. These tragedies are called urbicide, and there are other examples. During different wars, these cities were brutally killed, murdered.

Consider Iraq, ignoring for the moment Afghanistan, Syria, and Libya. After the US invasion and occupation of Iraq in 2003, no sovereign controlled or protected the people of Iraq. Hundreds of thousands of civilians were killed; millions were forced to leave their homes. With a mixture of charismatic legitimacy and tribal authority based on fear and the cruelty of despotic actions, Saddam Hussein ruled Iraq. After the invasion, Iraq lacked a sovereign. Which, though, was better? A stable state charismatically ruled by a cruel dictatorship or a violent, anomic state occupied by foreigners lacking entitlement to authority? Although life was difficult, especially for dissidents and the Kurdish minority, life under Hussein was better in terms of meeting the basic requirements of everyday life. There was not only a factual order but also a normative order, a set of civic and legal norms. An educated, modern middle class, one of the most sophisticated in the Arab world, provided stability to the state. This middle class was the backbone of the state. After the US invasion, Iraq became a failed state. It became a puppet of the United States and is still trying to recover (Bacevich 2016; Fassihi 2008;

Filkins 2008; Otterman and Hill 2010; Schwartz 2008). The situation is similar in Afghanistan, Syria, and Libya.

It is possible to kill a nation of people. Remember the Holocaust and the murder of six million European Jews, the Khmer Rouge in Cambodia where one million Cambodians were slaughtered, the Bangladesh genocide in 1971 when hundreds of thousands of people were killed and hundreds of thousands women raped, the genocide in Srebrenica under the promised protection of the United Nations, Rawanda when 800,000 were massacred in 100 days, the native population in Newfoundland, Canada, called Beothuks, entirely erased in the 1800s, and the Rohingya today in Myanmar. To murder an entire nation of people is genocide.

Is it possible, however, to kill society? What would it mean to kill society? Is there something within society that is resistant to its demise? Whenever human beings gather, is there an unerasable part of their solidarity? If society were, in fact, killed, what is it that is actually being killed? Not inhabitants. Not material culture. What would be killed would be trust in a normative orientation to provide security to members of the community. Human beings would exist together in an utterly asocial situation, a state of nature.

Jose Saramago's novel *Blindness* (1997) dramatizes the death of society. Everyone except one person loses their sight. There are human beings, but they do not live together as a society. They gather as a pack. The novel depicts the unchecked destructive instinct at a collective level. Blindness is Saramago's trope for the absence of the social with the dark demise of government and every social institution. In this most anomic situation, however, a burial ceremony occurs for a woman who was not loved but respected for no other reason than that she was a human being. This scene occuring at the climax of the novel depicts an ever-present social nature inherent in humans beings. Sightedness then slowly returns. Society resurrects itself.

Cormac McCarthy's popular *The Road* (2006) has a similar theme. Two characters, a father and a son, are unnamed throughout the novel. Their hopeless lives in a postapocalyptic world are starkly narrated. We never know their names. Without a society, there is not a reason to know another's name. Blindness was a trope for sociocide for Saramago. Anonymity is a trope for sociocide for McCarthy. While there are remnants and memories of the old society, no new society emerges to take its place. The dread and negative fear of the son and father are to be eaten by cannibals, who roam the countryside. When the father dies from sickness, the boy stays with him for three days and then leaves the father covered with a blanket, a burial ritual, that the boy has internalized as a social human being, and another man, one of the good ones, adopts the boy taking him home where he has other children. A community emerges after sociocide.

Dystopian literature as a genre is increasingly popular. Still another example is *Station Eleven* by Emily St. John Mandel (2014). The dystopian literature tacitly dramatizes the possibility of sociocide, in the case of *Station Eleven*, because of a deadly global pandemic. Sociocide is a limit that dystopian novels confront because if sociocide truly did occur, there would be no reason for humans to tell a story. To whom would one tell a story with the confidence that another would understand the story? There would be no social foundation upon which to tell a story. Stories, folklore, parables, legends, myths preserve the social; here is their essential function.

When the reality of a normative orientation that provides security to the people in the society is killed, there is sociocide. Such is the reality for the characters in Saramago's *Blindness,* McCarthy's *The Road*, and Mandel's *Station Eleven*. Let us review different normative orientations then. One articulated by Ronald Dworkin in *Justice for Hedgehogs* is justice. Dworkin provides a compelling liberal formulation of justice.

> No government is legitimate unless it subscribes to two reigning principles. First, it must show equal concern for the fate of every person over whom it claims dominion. Second, it must respect fully the responsibility and right of each person to decide for himself how to make something valuable of his life. (Dworkin 2013, 2)

Here justice is a normative orientation upon which modern society thrives. Justice is the normative orientation to which not only members of society are subject but also the government is subject.

Another normative orientation is the Golden Rule. Do unto others as you would have them do unto you. With this normative orientation one is called upon to treat others as one would wish others would treat oneself. Whenever one takes the role of the other, one takes the role of the other as one would wish the other to take one's own role. This reciprocity resides within the human being rather than outside. The measure originates within oneself. The Golden Rule establishes trust within a community, say, a healthy congregation. It operationalizes kindness vis-á-vis superficial niceness.

In sociology, normative orientations, however, are studied more with respect to their functionality in terms of preserving social order than with respect to their moral truth. The problem is, to what degree can a normative orientation provide social order if it does not at the same time reflect a moral truth? One such normative orientation, the most basic, is the Hobbesian social contract. When there is society, which the English philosopher Thomas Hobbes (1968) calls the Leviathan, force and fraud no longer dominate. Force and fraud are criminal. When they occur, there is a societal reaction. According to Hobbes's philosophy on the origins of society, in exchange for protection from force and fraud, people give up their "natural" right to use force and fraud. The exchange is foresighted. Without the exchange life is short, nasty, and brutish. When the exchange occurs within a collective, there is a society. Voila!

Society thus serves a purpose. Society is not really an end-in-itself for Hobbes. It does not have an innate being or inner essence. Its purpose and essence are external to itself. Society is a means to an end. Its character is thus its utilitarianism. When the Hobbesian social contract is in place, people live longer and more peacefully than they would in a violent, anomic state of nature. The exchange gives up the natural right to use force and fraud for the promise to be protected from force and fraud. The exchange is a "deal." It serves people's self-interest efficiently, more efficiently than trying to survive in the state of nature for the short term where everyone is using unchecked force and fraud to live longer and more pleasurably and life becomes short, nasty, and brutish. The question is whether the utilitarian character of the Hobbesian social contract has enough persuasive weight to influence rational people to cease using force and fraud in order to ensure peace and harmony (Parsons 1968). To guarantee its "deal," the Leviathan, employs its omnipotent power; this power becomes its authority in so far as it guarantees with force the social contract.

Consider this sentence from Hannah Arendt:

> Today the truth has come home: there is no protection in heaven or earth against bare murder, and a man can be driven at any moment from the streets and broad places once open to all. At long last, it has become clear that the "senseless freedom" of the individual merely paves the way for the senseless suffering of his entire people. (1944, 121)

During wars societies digress and become a state of nature; they become nonsocieties. The truth that Arendt describes happens in every war. The barbarity of such experiences is increasing in today's wars. If a society bears this exceedingly painful situation continuously, will it remain a society? Will a society be able to restore itself?

WARS TODAY

During his Commencement Address on June 10, 1963, to the graduating class of American University, President John F. Kennedy said, "The United States, as the world knows, will never start a war. We do not want a war. We do not now expect a war." Kennedy believed what he said at this moment and that Americans also believed what he said. He expressed an idealistic sentiment, a moral self-understanding he felt a majority of Americans shared with him. Nevertheless, Kennedy himself initiated the United States' involvement in the war in Vietnam sending military advisors to South Vietnam to fight communist North Vietnam.

Today we have to say that the United States starts wars. The world knows the United States starts wars. In an interview on June 18, 2011 with the *New York Times*, Defense Secretary Robert Gates referred to the distinction between wars of necessity and wars of choice. Wars of necessity are a matter of life or death. Either fight or die. Wars of choice, are different. A life and death situation does not grip wars of choice. Gates said, "I will always be an advocate in terms of wars of necessity. I am just much more cautious on wars of choice" (Gates cited in Shanker and Bumiller 2011). Wars of choice are chosen. Because of some utilitarian calculus, economic interest, or instrumental purpose that serves a state's political self-interest, wars of choice are the wars one starts.

Gates says that he is "more cautious on wars of choice." Gates is willing to start a war of choice for pragmatic, self-interested reasons, albeit cautiously. No categorical imperative stops him. Wars of choice remain an option. Kennedy indicated he was against the United States starting wars, undertaking wars of choice. Kennedy believed or wanted us to believe that the United States was better than that.

The problem is that wars of choice are reckless no matter how much caution is used in starting them. Wars of choice are morally banal, and it is important to understand why. In Plato's *Gorgias*, Socrates asks Polus whether it is worse to suffer wrong or to do wrong. Polus answers that it is worse to suffer wrong. Polus says that as an experience it is worse to suffer wrong than do wrong. Socrates then asks Polus whether it is more base to suffer wrong or to do wrong. We expect Polus to answer that it is less base to do wrong and more base to suffer wrong. Callicles, for example, argues, "The experience of suffering wrong does not happen to anyone who calls himself a man; it happens to a slave who had better die than live, seeing that when he is wronged and insulted he cannot defend himself or anyone else for whom he cares" (Plato 1971, 78). In the Platonic dialogue Polus surprises readers when he answers it is less base to suffer wrong and more base to do wrong. At this point, careful readers see that Polus does not need to be taught morality. Socratic reason is not needed. Polus already has a sense of morality (McKim 1988).

Wars of choice are based on the opposite conviction of Polus, namely, the conviction of natural right. The conviction of natural right, as Callicles describes, is that it is less base to do wrong and more base to suffer wrong, thus the decision to do wrong. Wars of choice choose to do wrong. This thinking informs the Bush doctrine which advocates preemptive strikes and unilateral military intervention, gradually amplified by the Obama and Trump administrations. Understandably, Gates is cautious with wars of choice.

Wars of choice are costly in terms of financial costs. The Iraq War cost three trillion dollars. They are immeasurably costly in terms of loss of human lives. "War-related Iraqi civilian deaths are estimated at anywhere between 180,000 and 1 million; 14 percent of Iraq's population (4 million) is displaced: 2 million people have been displaced within the country, 2 million are living as refugees in neighboring countries" (Fassihi 2008, 277). Wars disproportionately kill civilians, innocent children, women, and men. The Iraq War was a war of choice on the part of President George W. Bush. Bush later admitted publicly that there was no evidence linking Iraq to 9/11, the mendacious rationale Donald Rumsfeld, Dick Cheney, Colin Powell, and others offered to invade Iraq, a group which John W. Dower (2010, 105) says refers to itself as "the Vulcans." The war in Iraq was reckless. The war was morally banal and ethically unconscionable. The United States did wrong.

Wars create an anomic state of nature where force and fraud become the cardinal virtues. Wars demolish houses and the prestige of the home. Wars kill civilians and cities' traditions. Wars destroy communities and their history and collective memory. Wars eradicate social systems and society itself.

In "Perpetual Peace: A Philosophical Sketch," Immanuel Kant writes, "No state shall, during war, permit such acts of hostility which would make mutual confidence in the subsequent peace impossible" (1917, 114). Wars today are conducted in the exact opposite manner. Their purpose is to make trust in a subsequent peace impossible. Such acts of hostility are planned. This strategy fuels endless wars. This tactic perpetuates wars because agreement is undesirable. Since agreement is undesirable, force continues to decide between men and women. "Where war establishes the situation of force, the right ends" (Jaspers 2001, 31). Sociocide takes place.

In *The Phenomenology of Mind*, G. W. F. Hegel makes the opposite argument. He argues that war leads to the rejuvenation of society.

> In order not to let them (families, private communities) get rooted and settled in this isolation and thus break up the whole into fragments and let the common spirit evaporate, government has from time to time to shake them to the very centre by War. By this means it confounds the order that has been established and arranged, and violates their right to independence, while the individuals (who, being absorbed therein, get adrift from the whole, striving after inviolable self-existence and personal security), are made, by the task thus imposed on them by government, to feel the power of their lord and master, death. (1977, 443)

While Hegel says war restores society as a whole, this study argues war fragments society as a whole such that it is no longer society. While Hegel sees war preventing the common spirit from evaporating, this study sees war dispersing the common spirit.

Chapter Two

Sociocide and the US Invasion of Iraq

Coauthored with Jeffery Boucher

March 20, 2003—the United States of American launched Operation Iraqi Freedom. The media depicted the invasion as a quick and surprisingly successful military operation; simultaneously, American forces left a trail of social and moral resentment in the eyes of Iraqis and the observing world. After the invasion and occupation, no sovereignty controlled or protected the people of Iraq. Hundreds of thousands of civilians, yes, hundreds of thousands of civilians, were killed; millions forced to leave their homes. The invasion agitated an insurgency with sectarian violence that led to the rise and injustices of ISIS, not only in Iraq but in Syria. How wounded was the society of Iraq as a result of the US military occupancy? Why was Iraq's society unable to establish social order?

Trotsky said, "Every state is founded on force," but force alone, Max Weber (1947) insists, does not secure a state. Iraqis neither respected nor obeyed the factual power that the US occupiers asserted. When the force employed is not seen as legitimate, peace is out of reach. One reporter puts it this way, "If attaining true political authority depends on securing a monopoly of legitimate violence, then the Americans would never achieve this in Iraq" (Danner 2006). Warring parties, even powerful ones, were not able to claim a monopoly of legitimate violence. The American military never achieved the political authority with which to stop Iraq from falling into chaos. The American occupation continues with its political and military clout. The more the American military attempts to attain authority through force or through buying the loyalty of former enemies, the more the American military undermines the community that would grant such authority. The more the American military employs sheer force against the Iraq people, the more the United States loses legitimacy not only in Iraq but with other nations and former allies. The United States loses legitimacy within its own country as well.

Saddam Hussein was an oppressive dictator; he had the power to rule. He ruled with a mixture of charismatic legitimacy and traditional authority based on fear and the cruelty of his despotic actions. Hussein was sovereign. One question for Iraqis became: Which was better, a state charismatically ruled by dictatorship or a non-state occupied by unwanted foreign invaders? "I heard an educated Iraqi say today that if Saddam Hussein were allowed to run for elections, he would get the majority of the vote" (Fassihi 2008, 125). Before the invasion, life was difficult especially for dissidents and Kurds. Nevertheless, life was better with respect to meeting the requirements of everyday social life. There was a factual order as well as a normative order. An educated middle class, the most sophisticated and secular in the Arab world (unrecognized and unappreciated in the Western media) supported a modern civil society while ruled by a dictator.

After the invasion, Iraq suffered waves of sectarian violence.

> The leaders of the occupying forces could have avoided dismantling the state institutions, disbanding the army, and engaging in a de-Baathification campaign. They could have had a plan to deal with ethnic and religious conflict. They could have prepared themselves for the rising influence of Iran on the Shia majority that has come to power in Iraq. They could and should have refrained from arbitrarily arresting, humiliating, and torturing people. (Kis and Michnik 2008)

Did US leaders instigating the Iraq invasion (George W. Bush, Dick Cheney, Donald Rumsfeld, Colin Power, Condoleeza Rice, and Paul Wolfowitz) believe that after their invasion they could create a state ex nihil? Did all evidence of previous state structures and civil society need to be dismantled? Did the leaders of the American occupation think state institutions could be constructed based on nothing other than its foreign and capitalistic control?

It is not correct to say leaders of the American invasion occupation did not have a plan; it is better to say they lacked a plan that took into account the matter of legitimacy. Speaking to the realist perspective of the modern state that guided them, Theda Skocpol (1979, 31–32) explains this reasoning: "If state organizations cope with whatever tasks they already claim smoothly and efficiently, legitimacy—either in the sense of moral approval or in the probably much more usual sense of sheer acceptance of the status quo—will probably be accorded to the state's form and rulers by most groups in society." Leaders of the American occupation assumed legitimacy would be established through the Iraqis "sheer acceptance of the status quo." Skocpol (1979, 32) continues to account for this realist perspective, "Even after great loss of legitimacy has occurred, a state can remain quite stable—and certainly invulnerable to internal mass-based revolts—especially if its coercive organizations remain coherent and effective. . . . Such an analytic focus seems certain to prove more fruitful than any focus primarily or exclusively upon political legitimation." Skocpol's remark frames the political thinking of the leaders of the American occupation. When "coercive organizations remain coherent and effective," there is no need to focus on the question of legitimacy. The functional requirement of legitimacy for resolving conflict, however, cannot be understated. Skocpol's theorizing belies a fundamental truism in Max Weber's sociology, rejecting the significance of Weber's work. The example of the US invasion of Iraq suggests the need to revisit Weber's sociological account of legitimacy.

The US military destruction in Iraq transformed Iraq into a Hobbesian jungle, one the American military was unable to tame because it generated and participated in its creation and perpetuation. In *Waiting for an Ordinary Day: The Unraveling of Life in Iraq*, Fassihi writes, "For those of us on the ground, it's hard to imagine what, if anything, could salvage it from its violent downward spiral. . . . The war has cost the United States approximately three trillion dollars, and the effect of its psychological trauma on Americans and Iraqis is just beginning to surface" (2008, 277). In the Hobbesian jungle, life is nasty and painful, brutish and short. Unchecked violence everywhere means painful lives for everyone. In response to this unbearable condition, human beings, with their self-interest and their capacity for reason, cease to employ violence. Why? Violence no longer is an efficient means for meeting individuals' needs. After being in this situation for any length of time, people are compelled to establish a social contract to restrict each other's use of force and fraud. Herein is the purpose of the state. The basis for this modern social contract is utilitarian. Society here is a cognitive entity grounded in utilitarian logic. The Hobbesian social contract needs no moral truth or metaphysical principle to affirm it given its pragmatism. Society is a rational response to a painful experience, namely the war of all against all. People agree to be ruled by the power of the state in exchange for the state's promise and guarantee of security. The state, Hobbes's Leviathan, acquires a monopoly on the legitimate use force because its purpose, its authority, is to ensure social order, that is, stop individuals' capricious and random use of force and fraud.

After the invasion, Iraqis lived without a social contract. No sovereign insured social order. The US military could not replace Hussein. The horrors of the war and the manipulations of the United States prohibited a social contact from taking hold. The unpredictability and randomness of suicide bombings exemplified week after week that the US military, despite its power, lacked the authority to establish a sovereign state. The Iraq government was fragmented and deferent to its foreign occupancy; the puppet government not only failed but also perverted a sense of civic order. While it had been important to eliminate and dispose of Hussein symbolically, the task was pragmatically difficult given his successful hiding and politically awk-ward show trial and hanging. People fell back to tribal traditions, focusing on the Sunni and Shia branches of Islam, in a search for legitimacy in their lives, what Weber calls traditional authority. The modern state based on legal-rational authority was no longer viable, except on paper written by foreign-ers. In an effort to suppress the insurgency, the US military itself attempted to reach out to Iraq's traditional legitimacy based on tribal histories. The option was pursued because the members of Iraq's civil society and state bureaucracy, composed of officials from different ethnic and faith traditions within Iraq, abandoned the state, making it impossible to establish legal-rational legitimacy. Traditional authority was the last option left to the US military for restoring order with something other than force. The more the US military used sheer force alone, the more it fragmented the society of Iraq into a contentious set of mini-states with their own fiefdoms.

To understand the tragic consequences of the US invasion, it is necessary to raise the importance of legitimacy. "With no state to protect them, the Iraqis have, in fact reverted to the lowest common denominator: the tribe, the clan, and the neighborhood. It's a vicious circle: the foreign occupancy bars any stabilization of a state and the absence of a state perverts consideration of an end to the occupation" (Luizard 2008). The situation in Iraq remained fatalistic, and no progress could be made. The negativity of this double-bind made the situation hopeless for the society.

Authority and legitimacy become mute issues when there is no longer a society. Authority and legitimacy lose their raison d'etre. Giorgio Agambon (2000) theorizes this situation as a camp: "The camp is that space that opens up when the state of exception starts to become the rule." Iraq digressed into a camp, not just the prison camps that the US military established and in which prisoners were tortured, but the state itself. The state of exception, as the capricious rule and logic of force alone, operated independently of the rule of law. The short stories by the Iraq writer, Hassan Blasim, *The Corpse Exhibition: And Other Stories of Iraq* (2014), narrate this bleak life in a camp starkly. There are no friends. No enemies. No scapegoats. Nihilism rules gleefully. All are what Agamben call *homo sacer*, killed randomly, buried without ritual, not even cursed because there is no society to curse them. In the short stories, nihilism reigns and rules the life-world depicted.

If sociocide occurred within Iraq today, would it be because of some pathology within the society itself after years of despotic rule by Saddam Hussein? The American public wants to believe the violence in Iraq is reflec-tive of such a case. The violence in Iraq stems from its own pathological history. After the horrific war between Iraq and Iran from 1980 to 1988, there was an earthquake waiting to occur in Iraq. While it is true that every society has its fault line upon which an earthquake may occur, either natural or social, the American public does not want to recognize the consequences of its war in Iraq.

There are two ways to search for a "cause" of sociocide. Is the cause intrinsic or extrinsic? An individual may kill himself or herself due to some internal trauma. The killing may be induced from within. Likewise, sociocide may be induced by some trauma within the society. The xenophobia incited by the society's leader may lead to collective suicide. A historical example of a community committing suicide drinking poison together is Jonestown in Guyana in 1978. Interestingly, the community's collective suicide was not complete in that one individual escaped into the forest later to bear witness to the event. The xenophobia incited by President Trump may lead in the face of the pandemic to collective suicide in the United States, a matter more fully and carefully discussed in chapter 8.

Sociocide, however, could also be compared to domicide, urbicide, and genocide, where an outside agent, militia, group, or power destroys with lethal force a home, city, or nation of people. The violence is brought to bear from outside. Violence has been brought to bear against the states of Bosnia-Herzegovina, Chechnya, Syria, Afghanistan, Libya, and Iraq. This violence makes it difficult for these societies to continue as societies. If sociocide was occurring within Iraq, was it the result of the American military occupation? Was the United States responsible for the death of not only a state but also a society? What would such a criminal event mean morally, politically, and legally? While American citizens are not yet able to recognize or address such a question, it is certainly a subtext in media discussions. While genocide is a crime in international law, sociocide is neither recognized nor charged as being a crime. Indeed, who would have the authority to judge such a crime except God?

Sociocide is the killing of the moral conscience of not just one individual but every individual in a group. Not only one individual but every individual fails to take the role of not only the other but, more importantly, what George Herbert Mead (1956) called the generalized other. In *The Road,* the boy, the youngest and most innocent, never lost this moral conscience. He wanted to help the old traveler they met on the road, rescue the humans in a home who were to be eaten, and worried whether his father was no longer good after killing an attacker. It is a dramatic counterpoint to the anomic life in which his father and he try to survive. Even literature cannot sustain the illusion of sociocide without the social reemerging out of the merciless state of nature. When two or three are gathered together, the social arises. "When two or three are gathered together in his Name, you will be in the midst of them." This prayer is not just a theological truism; it is also a social truism.

Sociocide may not describe something that exists empirically. It may be best to be skeptical as to whether sociocide has ever taken place or whether sociocide even can take place. Sociocide then is a Weberian ideal type.

It is necessary for the sociologist to formulate pure ideal types of the corre-
sponding forms of action which in each case involve the highest possible
degree of logical integration by virtue of their complete adequacy of meaning.
But precisely because this is true, it is probably seldom if ever that a real
phenomenon can be found which corresponds exactly to one of these ideally
constructed pure types. (Weber 1947, 110)

What is sociocide as an ideal type? Weber says that "In no case does it refer
to an objectively 'correct' meaning or one which is 'true' in some metaphysical sense" (1947, 89). While sociocide may be true in some metaphysical
sense, think of Plato's Socratic discussion of the possibility of nothingness in
The Sophist, it does not refer to something empirically correct. As an ideal
type, it provides a meaningful degree of logical integration to account for the
perverse and demented character of modern wars. It offers not only descriptive but explanatory power.

One of the first scholarly uses of the term is by Johan Galtung (1982). In
his work, Galtung coins several terms, e.g., omnicide, femicide, ethnicide,
and ecocide. Galtung treats sociocide as a descriptive term to name the killing of the social just as omnicide would be a nuclear war that destroys the
entire earth. Galtung, though, does not formulate sociocide as an ideal type.

The term sociocide is close to the term, demodernization, which is used
by V. A. Tishkov in his anthropological study of war in Chechnya. Tishkov
(2005, 170) writes: "The situation in Chechnya is not one of rapid changes
with which society cannot cope, causing it to descend into a state of anomie,
but one of chaotic changes in which the very concept of society is swept
away. During the armed conflict the Chechen 'nation', and even Chechen
'society,' ceased to exist as an agent of social action." While describing what
demodernization is, Tishkov implicitly formulates what sociocide would be.
Tishkov indirectly provides an account of what sociocide would be. After
sociocide, society ceases to be an agent of social action. Individuals act and
act atomistically, no doubt within their families and small communities, but
society itself is not an agent of social action. Human beings live and live
together; society does not exist as an agent of social action

Tishkov distinguishes demodernization from sociocide. "Demodernization is thus a radical transformation of social links and institutions that undermines the otherwise universal capacity of human communities for self-organ-
ization. But it does not pitch society into a state of complete chaos. Rather it
retains the basic institutions of family and even local quasi-administrations,
though the latter is left severely eroded" (2005, 171). Demodernization represents a regression that stops before becoming the absolute destruction of the
social. While society has lost its universal capacity for human organization,
the basic institution of family remains. Sociocide would erase the basic insti-

tution of the family as well, as it almost did in *The Road* where the father and son appeared to be the last surviving family.

Sociocide would be the consequence at the collective level of what Sigmund Freud calls the destructive instinct, which turns "what is living into an inorganic state." Eros, in contrast, is the instinct of self-preservation or the preservation of the human species in an organic state. Sociocide results in the destruction of the human species as an organic being. Sociocide turns what is living into an inorganic state, it is the energy of necrophilia. Freud notes, "We are without a term analogous to libido for describing the energy of the destructive instinct" (Freud 1949, 19). Sociocide is provided here as the word that would the appropriate term for the energy of the death instinct, which dystopian literature dramatizes as its antagonist.

We need here to distinguish sociocide from anomie, which is difficult because the two concepts run into each other and appear interchangeable. Anomie is the loss of society's collective ego, what George Herbert Mead would call "the generalized other." During anomie, there is no "generalized other" whose role a member can take. While there may be individual or group behaviors, there is no social action in the full sense of the word. There are no normative orientations or collective values around which action can be purposeful. Randomness replaces all normative orientations and becomes itself the dominate normative orientation. The hegemony of randomness is absolute. Anomie exists when there is only society's libido and no collective ego. Sociocide would be different. With sociocide there is no libido. There is the antithesis of the libido; there is the death instinct, which turns the social into the mechanical and the transcendent into the concrete.

With sociocide, Plato's Divided Line would collapse. The consequence of sociocide is that nothing from the realm of the sensible passes to the realm of ideas and nothing from empirical reality into the conceptual realm. Transcendental understanding becomes an illusion, understanding opaque, which is why earlier we said that the possibility of telling stories would no longer exist.

If our interest is to understand what sociocide would be, it is helpful to try to imagine what human life together would be like after sociocide. As mentioned, the political theorizing of Giorgio Agamben (2000) imagines the possibility of sociocide. As a result of sociocide, people would no longer live in a society but in a camp. Whether it be a city or entire country, in this camp human beings could not be murdered or even sacrificed as scapegoats. There would be no society to understand their deaths in such terms. They simply would be killed, and their status would be that of a *homo sacer*. Their burial would be not only gratuitous but banned. Saramago's novel, however, depicts how even in the most anomic circumstances a burial occurs, indeed even for ones who may not be loved but who are respected. Who would ban the funerals of these killed human beings if there indeed were no society?

Has the society of Iraq been fatally killed? We are skeptical as to whether sociocide has actually taken place. Although the society in Iraq as a living organism is deeply distraught and profoundly traumatized, there is still solidarity between humans. A comparable example of this point is found in Svetlana Broz's *Good People in an Evil Time* (2004), which provides testimonies of how during extreme and unconscionable violence in Bosnia people from different ethnic groups preserved across ethic boundaries good will, trust, and friendship. Under the most brutal circumstances there remained a remnant of the social. Although it seems possible to murder a society, and some may argue that such has actually happened at various times in history, society has a kind of immortal character. There is in humanity an unfathomable sense of interrelatedness and interconnectedness. There is a resiliency based on what the human species-being is and on who human beings are as individuals and members of a community—this is the subtle backbone of the social.

Chapter Three

The Ethical Requirement of Burial, Humanity, and Its Transgression

Classical Anthropology Applied

During the war against Bosnia, the Bosnian Serb and Yugoslav People's Army targeted civilian funerals. During funeral services, massacres occurred. The shelling prevented family members from burying loved ones and forced communities to abandon their deceased in fields or on streets. The aggressors discarded the bodies into pits or mines. The term, "mass graves," is a misnomer because mass graves are not graves. Religious ceremonies are not performed; social rituals do not take place. In Sarajevo Serbian snipers even shot at and killed men preparing graves. Religious leaders took refuge leaping into graves while saying prayers for the dead. Snipers wounded children and women while throwing dirt into a grave during funerals (Kapić 2000, 238).

What is the evil in war crimes? The words evil and war crimes are just words, signifiers. One needs to recover what these signifiers signify. Otherwise, the words lose their meaning despite the preponderance of their use. It helps at this point to review the ritual that is transgressed, namely, the burial, by revisiting the relevant literature in classical anthropology. Since the dawn of society, humans have conducted burials. Even if in modern times men and women do not ponder the meaningfulness of the ritual, as long as there is a society, even an atheistic society, the ritual occurs. The burial sustains the social. The anthropologist Clyde Kluckhohn defines a funeral as "a symbolic assertion that a person is important not only to his immediate relatives but to the whole group" (1964, 136). The funeral is a ritual. A ritual is a symbolic assertion. However the ritual may be conducted (as anthropology shows us there are innumerable ways), funerals are symbolic rituals that reflect cultural patterns, historical traditions, and social practices.

In *The Siege of Sarajevo: 1992–1996*, Vlado Raguz, Director of the Funeral Services Company of Sarajavo, tells how formidable it was to provide funerals for the dead. Coffins were not available, and so wardrobes were used. To transport the deceased from their homes to the mortuary and then the cemetery, petrol had to be purchased from black marketers at thirty Deutsche Mark a liter. Nevertheless, 15,000 people were buried with funeral ceremonies during the siege under impossible circumstances in Sarajevo (Kapić 2000, 726). The people of Sarajevo and their community bear witness to this unrecognized human achievement. During the siege, the city retained its ethical spirit and character despite the vicious circumstances and despite the world's betrayal of the city.

The sociologist Emile Durkheim says that, "It is no longer out of affection that we mourn the dead, it is out of duty" (1975, 15). Emotional trauma and social instability are components of the human burial. The funeral provides comfort during times of extreme emotional distress; the funeral reassures the community of continuity after suffering profound loss. But, ultimately, it is duty, ethical duty, that makes the burial rite necessary for individuals as well as society; that is, the funeral exemplifies the ethical spirit of the human species, something not shared and so essentially different from other species of the animal world. While death traumatizes a collective of animals, animals (elephants, orangutans, chimpanzees, magpies) do not utilize symbolic rituals to bury their deceased.

Journalists depicted conditions in Bosnia as analogous to a Hobbesian jungle. The story line was "Might is right" and "Every man for himself." Social duty, the media indicated, was difficult to find. Sarajevo, however, did not digress into a Hobbesian presocial state of "a war of all against all." The fact that 15,000 people were provided funeral services despite sadistic conditions supports this point. The ethical spirit of the community persevered. The community remained intact. The social fabric of the community was not shredded, despite every effort to do so.

Human burials have historical significance; empirically, they serve as historical markers for the birth of society (Solecki 1971). Human burials exemplify recognition of the distinctiveness of the human species in relation to other species. In the evolutionary history of the human species, the burial is the first meaningful ritual. The ritual demarcates the human species as what it is. Herein lies the ethical content of the human burial. The burial, not death, acknowledges who human beings are. The burial, not death, defines the human being.

In performing the burial rite, human beings are not merely conscious of their life-activity. They are not merely one with their life-activity as animals are one with their life-activity. They instead are self-conscious, and this self-consciousness is what distinguishes human beings as a distinct species-being. Karl Marx (2004, 35) writes, "But man makes his life-activity itself an object of his will and consciousness. He has a conscious life-activity. . . . Conscious life-activity distinguishes man from the life-activity of animals." Conscious life-activity means the human being is capable of being both collectively conscious and individually conscious. During the burial ceremony, the life-activity of the individual and the life-activity of the community in relation to the individual become the object of reflection. The burial ritual represents the human species, its inherent and essential self-consciousness.

Human beings are impelled to take special action in the face of death. On this point, the anthropologist A. L. Kroeber writes:

> When prehistoric skeletons are found in the position in which death might take place, the presumption is that the people of that time abandoned their dead as animals would. If, on the other hand, a skeleton lies intact with its arms carefully folded, there is little room for doubt human beings had arrived at a crude recognition of the difference between flesh and spirit. (1923, 171)

Human beings do not ignore the cessation of activity and the lapse of consciousness that accompanies death. Human beings are impelled to take special action, and this point is dramatized in the novels mentioned earlier, *Blindness* and *The Road*. During the most anomic situation in *Blindness*, a burial ceremony occurs for a woman for no other reason than that she was a human being. This scene becomes the novel's turning point depicting human beings innate social nature. When the father dies in *The Road*, the boy stays by him for three days and then leaves the father after covering him with a blanket, which is the boy's manner of performing a burial rite as a human being without any community. This action leads to him joining a community.

Kroeber theorizes on this matter, "Even to say that Neanderthal man did not know whether his dead were dead implies his recognition of something different from life in the body, for he recognized, of course, that the body had become different" (1923, 171). Consider how this point is exemplified by the Tutsi survivors reporting how it was that they survived while being hunted daily in the hills like wild animals over several months. The Tutsi survivors narrate what it meant for their social relations to the ones who were killed during the Hutu's genocide against Tutsi. Berthe Mwanankabandiin in Jean Hatzfeld's *The Antelope's Strategy: Living in Rwanda after the Genocide* (2009, 101) says:

> There was no pity for the dead in the marshes. Nobody thought about burying them, there were too many of them, we couldn't possibly. The sight of their nudity touched us in a horrifying way: those bodies hardly reminded us at all anymore of living people. We didn't bother with ceremonies for the unlucky ones who'd been cut; we simply said they'd been unlucky. Death was an

everyday thing, from morning till night, so we no longer paid attention to the fate of corpses. Naturally, we might happen to spread a bit of mud over one of them, an acquaintance or a relative, but as to the others, we were too over-whelmed to deal with them.

The genocide became sociocide, killing the self-consciousness of the individuals in the community, their human species-being. Sociocide, however, did not occur. The Tutsi, who were hunted every day all day, would sometimes stop and "spread a bit of mud over" someone who had been cut and killed. This minimalist act was powerful; it mimed a burial ritual. It witnessed the immortality of the human species-being.

One survivor reflects, "The genocide killed off the sanctity of death in Rwanda." In order to restore the sanctity of death, the dignity of the burial ritual needed to be restored. One survivor testifies:

> We buried casually, without digging deep, without gathering flowers, without putting on a pretty dress. We felt freed from death. Then the foreigners came to help us. Humanitarian workers taught us to reconsider the remains of our families murdered in the swamps, imagining them as normal bodies. They drew us into funeral processions; they taught us modern attitudes of humanity, and reinstated elaborate ceremonies. They pushed us, as if they feared we would never again give a spit about the terrifying power of death. (Hatzfeld 2009, 102)

These funerals were necessary to recover not only from genocide but also from sociocide. It required the intervention of foreigners because it was not possible for the community itself to revive the funeral ceremony.

The philosopher G. W. F. Hegel formulates the tension between the empirical and theological understanding of the human burial and in a dialectical manner reconciles their tension. With the burial service, the right of consciousness asserts itself over and against nature. With the funeral prayer, "You are dust and to dust you shall return," the right of nature over the deceased, over the flesh of the deceased, is granted. At the same time, the prayer denies nature its right to subsume the person. The prayer denies nature its right to subsume the spirit of the person. "You are dust and to dust you shall return" lifts the spirit of the person out of the clutches of nature even as it grants nature its claim to the body of the deceased. G. W. F. Hegel writes lucidly on this expression of the ethical spirit of the human species, an ethical spirit expressed in every culture in every historical period.

> The family keeps away from the dead this dishonoring of him by the desires of unconscious organic agencies and by abstract elements, puts its own action in place of theirs, and weds the relative to the bosom of the earth, the elemental individuality that passes not away. Thereby the family makes the dead a member of a community which prevails over and holds under control the powers of

the particular material elements and the lower living creatures, which sought to have their way with the dead and destroy him. (1977, 472)

The disposal of the corpse has never been a matter of expedience or practical function.

Kluckhohn explains why this is so: "It is truly amazing that no known group has ever adopted the functionally simplest mode of disposing of its dead—merely abandoning corpses or disposing of them without a rite of any sort" (1964, 134). The very phrase, "disposal of the corpse," belies the symbolic action that must accompany the burial. With varying degrees of complexity and religious concerns, the burial ritual is performed, but there is always a ritual, a ritual whose content shows dignity and respect for the individual as well as the human species of which the individual is a part.

What, then, does it mean to transgress violently and sadistically this inviolable burial ritual? Why is the transgression evil? In the video documentary, *We Are All Neighbors* (Christie 1992), narrated by the cultural anthropologist Tone Bringa, author of *Being Muslim the Bosnian Way*, there is this report from a Bosnian refugee within her own country.

> "All slaughtered. No one was left alive. They set fire to everything that was good in our lives. Everything destroyed . . . everyone slaughtered and killed. They didn't allow us to bury the dead. They were left."
> "Not allowed to bury the dead?"
> "No. Some tried to bury their relatives, but they couldn't. Three days they tried, got wounded, but they wouldn't let them. So, the bodies decomposed in the streets and in the fields. That's how it is."

This horrific experience occurred not only during the war in Bosnia, but also during recent wars in Iraq, Syria, Afghanistan, and other places. The experience has been neither adequately reported nor adequately addressed. Evil is not an abstract concept. Crimes against humanity are not a mere slogan. Evil is socially constructed in everyday life and directly experienced by human beings. The evil described is odious.

The goal of sociocide is to destroy humanity. Sociocide achieves its purpose by claiming not just that one person is a nonhuman being, but that the notion of humanity as a positive one is nonexistent. Evil relativizes the notion of humanity and mocks its significance. If sociocide were successful, humanity would lose its capacity to be itself; humanity would lose its capacity to make either itself or its members whole, which is the function of humanity. At such points, humanity's absence becomes conspicuous which, in the end, provokes humanity's imminent return. Humanity is resilient in ways that cannot be grasped empirically. The disassociation which sociocide seeks is never fully realized. The spirit of humanity prevents humanity from disassociating from itself absolutely.

The crime against her humanity that the refugee in Bosnia reports is not merely a matter of preventing the family from burying its dead. The crime against her humanity is a matter of forcing a family to abandon its dead despite the family's making every effort and taking every risk to do otherwise. Duty requires the family to provide a burial for its dead, and this duty is immutable even if it puts the family in harm's way.

The exercise of this duty represents the ethical spirit of the human species, something innate in every family. This ethical spirit, in turn, represents the backbone of the community. If the family is unable to perform this duty, a sense of remorse arises. No matter how blameless the family is, if a funeral ceremony for a loved one did not occur, there is a feeling of profound regret. This remorse does not reflect the absence of the ethical spirit in the family. Indeed, the opposite is true. The deeper the ethical spirit within the family, the deeper the remorse if the family is unable to bury a loved one.

A Cry from the Grave (Woodhead 1999), produced by the British Broadcasting Company, depicts poignantly the issue discussed here. After 8,000 Bosnian Muslim men and young boys were slaughtered and discarded in primary grave sites, their remains were secretly dug up with backhoes and their decomposing bodies transported to secondary locations. On this matter, Sarah Wagner (2008, 84) writes, "The Bosnian Serbs have surpassed even [the Nazis' technology of mass killing], not in their mastery of execution, but in their manner of defiling the initial burial sites." Sometimes a single disarticulated corpse would be found in multiple secondary sites.

The survivors of the genocide at Srebrenica on July 1995 are caught in a double-bind. Part of genocide as a crime against humanity is to obstruct the victims' families and community from burying the human beings who were wantonly murdered. A funeral preserves the memory and restores the significance of the murdered lives within a community. To carry out a funeral ceremony, however, identification of the decomposed human remains found at mass grave sites needs to occur. The longer the identification process takes, the harder it is for survivors of the genocide to carry out their duty to lost loved ones. While family members yearn to perform their duty, the family cannot if the remains of the deceased are neither recovered nor identified. The survivors are thus twice abused. Not only have they suffered the injustice of genocide and the betrayal of the international community, but they are also prevented from carrying out their family's ethical responsibility, a natural duty that will not go away with time or forced relocation.

There is a pressing need to identify the remains of the deceased, and it helps to recognize the reason for the intensive but still inadequate labor that goes into meeting this need after the genocide in Srebrenica. The ethical spirit of the family is stymied; it yearns to perform its duty for the dead, but it cannot if the remains of the deceased are not first identified. A radical feature of the war crimes in Bosnia was the aggressors' effort to make it impossible to recover the remains of the dead. These efforts perpetuated the sociocidal nature of the war crimes. The victims are twice abused, twice victimized. Jonathan Schell writes, "It lays a special obligation on the people of the future to deal with the crime, even long after its perpetrators are themselves dead" (1982, 161).

In the work, *Magic, Science, and Religion*, the anthropologist Bronislaw Malinowski makes this point: "In the tending of the corpse . . . the nearest relatives . . . always show horror and fear mingled with pious love, but never do the negative elements appear alone or even dominate" (1954, 48). With the burial ritual, the negative element of fear and horror never appear alone, never dominate. The negative element is countered by a positive element inherent in the burial ritual. The negative element is countered by the element of pious love. This is the positive and dominate content of the burial ritual.

Durkheim says in *The Elementary Forms of Religious Life* that "it is because rites serve to remake individuals and groups morally that they are believed to have a power over things" (1915, 370), and the point reinforces the argument here. The crime of genocide that occurred in Bosnia was not only the murdering of countless civilians. The crime was also the attempt to create a strictly negative response, a response only of horror and fear, to death within the family and to allow this negative response to dominate completely. The crime of genocide was the attempt to destroy the family by violating the inviolate duty of the family. If a family believes it has forsaken its ethical duty to its loved ones, the family has trouble recovering from its loss. Through no fault of its own, the family lapses into fear for its very being. In the attempt to make it impossible for families to continue as families, no matter where they came to be located, there is evil. This point is critical from the viewpoint of rebuilding civil society, reasserting morality, and restoring religion.

Genocide may be an insufficient term to describe the activity and consequences of the violence that takes place during wars. As powerful as the term is, genocide may not fully encompass the true character of war crimes today. Schell indicates how genocide leads to sociocide: "When crimes are of a certain magnitude and character, they nullify our power to respond to them adequately because they smash the human context in which human losses normally acquire their meaning for us" (1982, 145). The society is the human context in which human losses acquire meaning for us; to destroy the human context in which human losses acquire meaning is to destroy society. Schell continues: "Evil becomes radical whenever it goes beyond destroying individual victims (in whatever numbers) and, in addition, mutilates or destroys the *world* that can in some way respond to—and thus in some measure redeem—the deaths suffered" (1982, 145). Sociocide represents radical evil because sociocide seeks to mutilate the world that can respond to the deaths suffered and to destroy the life-world that in some measure redeems the deaths suffered.

Let us turn to a comparable situation from the war in Iraq. After the US invasion of Iraq, everyday hundreds of civilians fell victim to sectarian violence or bombing campaigns. Violence was a ubiquitous condition in the life of Iraqis. The number of dead civilians fluctuated with the waves of violence. The remains of Iraqi civilians are carried out of bombing ruins, pulled out of the sewers or dragged out of rivers. As one CNN report described, the many bodies are "so mangled and charred, they're unidentifiable" (Edwards and Juliano 2007).

The unidentified corpses of Baghdad were brought to the city morgue. It is here that many family members came to search for their lost love ones. During the bloodiest days of the war, thousands of bodies were being brought in each month. This number dropped, but the fact was that bodies still kept coming. The Baghdad morgue had set up a viewing room where families desperately kept their eyes locked onto a computer screen. "Photos show blue-faced men who have been handcuffed, gagged and tortured. Headless corpses and limbs. Bulging eyes. Bullet holes. Charred faces, frozen in a scream" (Bruce 2008). The photos were gruesome and disturbing, but they were a last hope for many hopeless family members.

The morgue itself only had three freezers, and it was only meant to hold 100 bodies. The numbers brought in pushed the city morgue well past capacity. Before the war, the city morgue only saw about seventy bodies a month; after the invasion scores of bodies continued to trickle in each week. The bodies just kept on coming, and the families searching for these lost souls did not stop. One Interior Ministry worker explains, "Everyday people come to me. I listen to their stories. People are in pain. They say 'We know he is dead. We just want to bury him'" (Tavernise 2005). This is why so many distraught family members make their way to the viewing room at the Baghdad city morgue. Despite this grim reality, the families are compelled to bury their dead.

There is an incredibly strong duty to bury the dead. In most cases this should not be a hard thing to do, but in Baghdad, many families were being driven away from the morgue. For these family members their chance of finding their dead decreased significantly. The cause of this is sectarian violence. Shiite militias used death threats and kidnappings to deter Sunnis from going to the morgue. This violence against the Sunnis was once held under control under Saddam's regime, but the violence and hatred returned. Sunnis were forced to go to extremes to find their dead. Some sent their Shiite friends to the morgue; others attempted to make it to the morgue, but some just gave up hope. Visiting the morgue as one Sunni explains is "an act of moral necessity and tradition" (Semple 2006). This necessity, he thought, was worth the risk to his own life. This was the cost of giving his family member a proper burial.

In Iraq, a group of Shiite volunteers led by Sheik Jamal al-Sudani took it upon themselves to take care of these unidentifiable corpses. As each month hundreds of bodies are left unclaimed, al-Sudani and his followers recovered these bodies and provided them a proper burial. The bodies are taken 150 miles from Baghdad to the city of Najaf. It is in this final resting place that graves are dug by hand. The dead are cataloged and photographed before they are put down to eternal rest. These volunteers go through a great deal of danger making sure the bodies of all religions receive a traditional Muslim burial that is dignified. As al-Sudani put it, "I look to them as human beings with it my duty to bury them so their sanctuary will not be violated again after the violation of their killing" (Edwards and Juliano 2007). This is why al-Sudani and his group have been burying unidentified dead for over twenty years, but things are now much worse than during the rule of Saddam Hussein. During the most oppressive years of Saddam, this group of volunteers was only burying up to forty bodies each month. During the worse days of this unconscionable war, al-Sudani and his group have buried up to 2,000 bodies in a month. In an interview, al-Sudani said, "Now you see Iraqi's houses, meant to be a family's safest place, have become like graves for their family members, because any minute, any second, they're ready to die by explosion, airstrikes or car bombs. And no man, and no government, American or Iraqi, can fix it because now that will take a miracle" (Edwards and Juliano 2007).

Can this be? Is there something immortal about society? Comments from Malinowski (1954, 53) help answer this question.

> We have seen already how religion, by sacralizing and thus standardizing the other set of impulses, bestows on man the gift of mental integrity. . . . In all this religion counteracts the centrifugal forces of fear, dismay, demoralization, and provides the most powerful means of reintegration of the group's shaken solidarity and of the re-establishment of its morale. . . . Religion here assures the victory of tradition and culture over the mere negative response of thwarted instinct.

It would be wrong to say that during the war, the observing world saw only the fearful and horrific conditions of the war. The observing world also witnessed what Malinowski calls the gift of mental integrity in the actions of a country's inhabitants, especially among everyday citizens. Human beings survive unconscionable wars, and they survive it with the gift of mental integrity. War journalists witnessed and reported this gift of mental integrity, a gift inherited from the various religious traditions and cultural customs of the countries in which wars occur. Some from the observing world deeply admired the gift of mental integrity that was depicted. Some also lamented the absence of this gift of mental integrity within their own communities and among world leaders responding to and participating in these sociocidal wars.

Chapter Four

The Iron Cage of Surreality

A Foucaultian Analysis of the Dayton Accords

The manifest function of the Dayton Accords was to stop the sociocidal war in Bosnia-Herzegovina, a war that was killing the country. The Dayton Accords stopped the sociocidal war, which is why the Dayton Accords is praised as one of the most important diplomatic achievements in our times. The war was unconscionable and immoral bringing deaths and horrific consequences to the lives of many and their communities. The genocide in Srebrenica stood as the ignoble pinnacle of this war, but some argue, and this author agrees, genocide was occuring in the pogroms in other areas such as Foča and Prijedor of Bosnia-Herzegovina at the very beginning of the war although the pogroms are not described as genocide.

During the drafting of the Dayton Accords, emergency measures regarding the inflated rights of three ethnic groups as a constituent peoples were taken. The Dayton Accords froze the war it stopped. While the Dayton Accords were meant to be a transitional tool, their latent function has been to leave the country politically stagnant for over twenty years. Unfortunately, the latent function supplanted the manifest one. The unanticipated consequence of the Dayton Accords is the death of Bosnia-Herzegovina as a unitary country. The Dayton Accords empower the ethnopoliticians to continue their sociocidal actions against the country. In other words, the Dayton Accords enables nationalists in each ethnic group to complete the socially lethal project which the war started.

This chapter uses the work of Michel Foucault to structure its critique of the Dayton Accords. It is helpful to keep in mind that the founders of postmodernism—Michel Foucault, Jean-Francois Lyotard, and Jacques Derrida—are admirers of the ancient Sophists. Foucault resents the "reassuring dialectic" Socrates employs to refute his ancient friends. Foucault believed that, if he were to encounter Socrates, he—unlike his ancient friends—would remain firm in his defense of sophistry and antipathy toward the moral principles in Platonic philosophy. Foucault's postmodern political philosophy helps us formulate and deeply critique the complex structure of the Dayton Accords and its sociocidal impact on a country.

If, after sociocide, society becomes a corpse, the state assumes a specific character. Foucault (1978, 102) describes this character: "It is a question of orienting ourselves to a conception of power which replaces the privilege of the law with the viewpoint of the objective, the privilege of prohibition with the viewpoint of tactical efficacy, the privilege of sovereignty with the analysis of a multiple and mobile field of force relations, wherein far-reaching but never completely stable, effects of domination are produced." The purpose of the state is to protect humans with the privilege of law, whether it be traditional or legal-rational. The function of the state is to limit sociability with the privilege of prohibition. The goal of the state is to stabilize society with the privilege of sovereignty. If sociocide were to occur, these actions of the state would cease and no longer have a purpose.

After sociocide, the power of the state is found instead in the viewpoint of the objective, the viewpoint of tactical efficacy, and "a multiple and mobile field of force relations, wherein far-reaching but never completely stable, effects of domination are produced" (Foucault 1978, 102). In other words, the state mimes the state of nature. There is no state, not even a failed state.

In November 1995, the Dayton Accords stopped the war in Bosnia-Herzegovina. A General Framework Agreement for Peace signed in Dayton, Ohio, framed Bosnia-Herzegovina as a single country made up of two different entities: the Federation of Bosnia-Herzegovina and the Republika Srpska, which are tantamount to mini-states within one country. Nationalist leaders (two of whom, Franjo Tuđman and Slobodan Milošević, were war criminals in the war they themselves started) ratified the Dayton Accords. Nikola Kovač (2007), ambassador to France for Bosnia-Herzegovina during the war, notes, "The international community tolerated the initiators of conflict and took the side of the stronger (not the victim), in the belief that the 'lords of war' were the only interlocutors." A state with two entities, three constitutive peoples, one district, ten cantons, and a rotating tripartite presidency was established.

Like Slovenia, Croatia, Serbia, Montenegro, and Macedonia, Bosnia-Herzegovina was a republic of former-Yugoslavia. The Dayton Accords establishes a rigid, iron cage, bureaucratic structure for a polyethnic society. Using the paradox of the fish soup, Francesco Palermo (2016, 160) characterizes the attempt this way: "It is relatively easy to turn an aquarium into a fish soup, but it is impossible to do the opposite . . . once a multiethnic society has exploded and conflicts have erupted, it is utopian to expect legal instruments to re-establish it." Political commentators point out that other Yugoslav republics had monolithic ethnic identities upon which to structure seemingly stable nation-states: The inhabitants of Croatia are mainly Croats, although not all; the inhabitants of Slovenia are mainly Slovens, although not all; and the inhabitants of Serbia are mainly Serbs, although not all. There are more than 200,000 Bosniaks who live in Serbia, Serbian Muslims.

Bosnia-Herzegoivna is primarily but not entirely composed of three ethnic groups: Bosnian Muslim, Bosnian Croat, and Bosnian Serb. Bosnian Muslims are a plurality. More than 10 percent of the country's inhabitants do not belong to any of these three ethnic groups. None of the three ethnic groups hold a majority as is the case in the other Yugoslav republics. Bosnia-Herzegovina is more of a polyethnic society than other republics, but this difference of degree should not mask the reality that other Yugoslav republics are also polyethnic societies. Yugoslavia held together its several polyethnic republics as one country.

In Yugoslavia, Bosnia-Herzegovina stood as a model for the other republics of a polyethnic solidarity. The Partisan formulation during the creation of Yugoslavia during World War II was "Without Bosnia there is no Yugoslavia and without Yugoslavia there is no Bosnia" (Palermo 2016, 159). Bosnia was called a mini-Yugoslavia. It might be just as well to say Yugoslavia was a macro-Bosnia. Palermo, however, turns this logic on its head; he asserts that "Multiethnic Bosnia has ceased to exist when multiethnic Yugoslavia collapsed" (2016, 159). If there is no Yugoslavia, then there is no Bosnia. Nationalists as well as international commentators use this faux rationalization to explain the cause for the war in Bosnia-Herzegovina that resulted in not only genocide but also sociocide.

Bosnia-Herzegovina, however, remains a polyethnic society albeit a deeply wounded one. The other former Yugoslav republics also remain polyethnic societies even after being established as independent nation-states. In Macedonia, a quarter of its citizens are Albanians, not South Slavs. It is wrongheaded to say that since Yugoslavia after the death of Tito could not remain a united country, neither could Bosnia-Herzegovina. Perhaps the paradox of the fish soup explains the collapse of Yugoslavia. The fish soup that was Yugoslavia cannot return to its original living aquarium. Bosnia, however, is still a living aquarium. Fish swim in the polyethnic aquarium. Ivo Banac (1993, 139) critiques the comparison of the collective identity of Yugoslavia with the collective identity of Bosnia-Herzegovina, noting how the difference is not one of degree but one of kind.

> If Bosnia were a collectivity of separate entities, then it would have been a mini Yugoslavia. But it is not that. Bosnia is a historical entity which has its own identity and its own history . . . I view Bosnia as primarily a functioning

society which Yugoslavia never was. My question is how does one keep a
complicated, complex identity like Bosnia-Herzegovina together?

It was a mistake for the international community to imagine the constitution
of Bosnia-Herzegovina could be structured like Switzerland's consociational
democracy. Bosnia-Herzegovina is an authentic polyethnic society, not a
formulaic multiethnic society. The Dayton Accords fail to keep a complicated, complex identity like Bosnia-Herzegovina together. They prevent a complicated, complex identity like Bosnia from remaining a united country, and
Foucault helps us see why and how.

Foucalt says that after sociocide the power of the state is found the viewpoint of the objective, the viewpoint of tactical efficiency, and an analysis of
"a multiple and mobile field of force relations, wherein far-reaching but
never completely stable, effects of domination are produced" (1978, 102).
We will carefully examine the postmodern power of the Dayton Accords in
light of each of Foucault's three assertions.

Objectivity is being positivistic for Foucault, absolutely concrete. A subject's value resides in the fact of its being an object. This epistemology is
comparable to surrealistic art. In a surrealistic painting, the subject's value
resides in the fact of its being an object. Beauty is the exact narration of its
object qua object, whether it be a dream or a concrete thing. There is meaning without understanding. There is understanding without meaning. When
Foucault says the power of the state is found in the viewpoint of the objective, he means the power of the state is found in its surreal sense of objectivity, where subject and object are fused.

The Dayton Accords insists on the "exact" or objective narration of the
ethnic composition of the country. The Dayton Accords classifies Bosniaks,
Croats, and Serbs as constituent peoples. The Dayton Accords not only ignores but also disenfranchises the greater than 10 percent of the citizens in
the country who are not members of one of these ethnic groups and who are
labelled Other. Participation in both the House of Representatives and the
House of Peoples, the two chambers of the state's parliament, as well as the
presidency is restricted to members of these three ethnic groups and regulat-
ed on the basis of a balanced representation between the three ethnic groups.
Ethnic ratio and rotation inform the presidential body of the country, and this
is called the collective presidency constituted by three members, each repre-
senting one of the three ethnic groups. Two members of the collective presidency cannot be from the same ethnic group. Each member of the collective
presidency from a different ethnic group then rotates as president of the
country.

To make the matter still even more exact and objective, these three presidents are selected from the two entities: the Federation of Bosnia-Herzegovina and the Republika Srpska. The two entities are a result of the ethnic

cleansing of territories during the war from 1992–1995 erasing centuries of a historical polyethnic heritage. The two entities were violently and sadistically established and ahistorically and artificially affirmed by the Dayton Accords. According to the Dayton Accords, for example, a Bosnian Serb living in the Federation of Bosnia-Herzegovina rather than the Republika Srpska cannot be a candidate for the country's presidency; only a Bosnian Serb living in Republika Srpska can be a candidate for the country's presidency. Moreover, the Bosnian Serb living in the Federation can only vote for the Bosnian Serb living in Republika Srpska who is running for the presidency. The status of the Bosnian Serb living in the Federation is Other as is the status of the greater than 10 percent of Bosnian citizens who are not members of one of the three major ethnic groups. The Dayton Accords discriminates against these people's political rights to equal and full citizenship. Likewise, a Bosniak or a Bosnian Croat living in Republika Srpska cannot be a member of the country's presidency. The status of the Bosniak or Bosnian Croat living in Republika Srpska, like the status of citizens who are not members of the three major ethnic groups, is Other.

To repeat, the Dayton Accords does not allow someone who is not a member of one of these three ethnic groups to be a member of either the National Parliament or the Presidency. The Dayton Accords violates the political rights of these Bosnian citizens who do not fall into one of the three largest ethnic categories. The Dayton Accords privileges the electoral advantage of ethno-politicians in each of the three ethnic groups (Mujkić 2008). Dervo Sejdić and Jakob Finci, Bosnians, who are Roma and Jewish, Bosnians who are neither Bosniak, Croat, or Serb and who are notable Bosnian citizens in terms of their civic responsibility, filed and won a law suit charging discrimination at the European Court of Human Rights. Nothing has changed more than ten years after Europe's highest human rights court condemned the Dayton Accords as discriminatory, giving citizens outside the three ethnic groups second-class status. The Dayton Accords gives meaning without understanding and understanding without meaning. The situation is surreal.

To reify this perversity, the Dayton Accords bans someone who does not wish to declare an ethnic identity from running for the country's highest office. Ms. Azra Zornić, like Dervo Sejdić and Jakob Finci, filed a case of political discrimination and human rights violation to the European Court of Human Rights and won her suit. Since Zornić refused to declare an ethnic identity and simply declared herself a citizen of Bosnia-Herzegovina, she is denied the right to run for the country's highest office. Her case is not mentioned as much as the one with Sejdić and Finci, and one reason may be because a woman rather than a man is suing. Her lawsuit, however, is more consequential and deeper in that she is suing on behalf of not her ethnicity and minority rights, but on behalf of her citizenship as a Bosnian which she shares with all Bosnians, the very political concept the Dayton Accords belies. The Dayton Accords insists on the "exact" narration of the ethnic composition of the country and in doing so it becomes disconnected with social reality and political truth. The category of Other trumps and then erases the category of citizenship in Bosnia-Herzegovina. The Dayton Accords operationalizes the "exact" and objective narration of the ethnic composition of the country, and the consequences is to discriminate against all citizens in the country (Dicosola 2016).

Richard Holbrooke, the US diplomat who was the main negotiator of the Dayton Accords, is often quoted as having said "the Dayton Accords is an imperfect peace." His mea culpa masks a deeper reality. The Dayton Accords is a perfectly imperfect peace. Its reality is irrational. Its rationality is surreal. The Dayton Accords eliminates any semblance of rational control over the political order and public discourse. The power of the Dayton Accords is found in its objective viewpoint that is antirational. Reason is liquidated.

This fragmentation of a polyethnic society with exact ratios occurs at the lower levels of government as well. In the Federation (vis-á-vis Republika Srpska), each of the three main ethnic groups are entitled to two positions among the six prominent positions in the Federation (the president of the Federation, the prime minister, the presidents of the two chambers of the Parliament, the president of the Appeal Court and the president of the Constitutional Course). The purpose is to insure an objectively balanced representation. When the distribution is not heeded, the government's decisions are challenged. This objectification itself becomes its own legitimacy, its own self-justifying legitimacy. The objectification is the legitimacy; the legitimacy is the objectification.

The Dayton Accords stands on a rigid, fossified positivism. The Dayton Accords stopped a horrific war, and its supporters argue that this realism justified the Dayton Accords and sustains its legitimacy, making it impenetrable to any moral criticism that is consequential and preventing the country's National Parliament from changing its constitution in light of the two successful lawsuits at the European Court of Human Rights charging discrimination. While the Dayton Accords appears to integrate the country and synthesize ethnic differences, it treats ethnic identities as discrete variables, as either black or white, as cue ball identities.

The anti-synthetic logos of the Dayton Accords is alien to the country it purports to hold together and actually breaks it apart. While religious traditions inform the ethnic differences in Bosnia-Herzegovina, their ethnic personalities are strongly based in overlapping and common cultures in everyday life. When the Dayton Accords reifies the religious identities of Bosnians and ignores their national personality, it keeps Bosnians separate and puts a void between them. Synthesis is not only impossible, but undesirable.The

Dayton Accords fails to recognize the deeper solidarity of this polyethnic society grounded in the principle of unity in diversity (Mahmutćehajić 2003).

The political intention of the Dayton Accords' architect was to protect the interests of the three largest ethnic groups, Bosniak, Croat, and Serb. The nationalistic leaders of the ethnic groups signed the Dayton Accords because they saw it as a way to protect their political interests. The Dayton Accords empowers the national-chauvinistic interests of each ethnic group. Now the ethnic groups are more fearful of each other, more defensive with each other, and more vulnerable to each other. The more than 10 percent of its citizens who are not members of these ethnic groups and who are labelled Other had their political rights to engage fully and equally in their country's governance taken away. Their ethnic identities, say, as Jewish or Roma, are treated as neutral and their minority rights denied.

Let us draw upon the second point that Foucault makes. The power of the state established by the Dayton Accords is found as well in the viewpoint of tactical efficacy. The term "constituent peoples" exemplifies tactical efficacy. Bosniacs are a constituent peoples; Croats are a constituent peoples; and Serbs are a constituent peoples. Constituent peoples means a group that belongs to a particular national identity. The term is tactical, that is, non-strategic, because "a citizen of Bosnia and Herzegovina is recognized only as a member of an ethnic group, and only through this recognition is he or she recognized as a member of a political community" (Mujkić 2008, 113). Constituent peoples is not strategic in terms of democracy because it erases the significance of the sum of the inhabitants that together comprise the citizens of the state. The Dayton Accords gives primacy to the constituent peoples and not the citizens of the state, who, as Azra Zornić shows us with her law suit, cannot engage fully, equally, and freely, in the governance of their country. The Dayton Accords gives autonomy to the constituent peoples, who show little responsibility toward the state but only toward themselves as constituent people, and no political responsibility to their fellow citizens. Citizenship becomes an empty identity whose status is subordinate to the category of Other. Citizens are sometimes not even assured of being able to attain a birth certificate for their children who are born in the country. The Dayton Accords leaves a bad situation unchanged because its substance is little more than the negative residue left after a sociocidal war. Moral principles are banished because the Dayton Accords fails to imagine a solidarity in a polyethnic society that is something other than utilitarianism.

To turn to Foucault's third point, the power of the state after sociocide becomes an analysis of "a multiple and mobile field of force relations, wherein far-reaching but never completely stable effects of domination are produced" (Foucault 1978, 102). On the one hand, the Dayton Accords offers a semblance of control for the state; on the other hand, it leaves the state with no control, no authority. It creates a country with two entities, three constitutive peoples, one district, ten cantons, and a rotating tripartite presidency, a system of government that is, not too complicated, but impossibly complicated. No country could function under this constitution. No people, no matter how peace loving, could coexist under the Dayton Accords. A state, by definition, is a political agent engaged in collective action for the good of the country. The Dayton Accords creates a state that is forced to be a non-state. Intelligence and discursive reasons are neutralized. Bad faith is rabidly and continuously reproduced in the public domaine and media, generating endless convulsive monologues among the ethno-politicians.

Palermo (2016, 164) writes, "As a mirror of Europe, Bosnia and Herzegovina reflects the image of Europe that Europe does not want to see. Both in sociopolitical and in legal terms. It reminds Europe of its past, of its present mistakes and insecurity as well as of its not unlikely future." To invert this point, Bosnia-Herzegovina reflects an image of Europe that Europe has not been since its early Middle Ages. The dominant kinship structure during the early Middle Ages in Europe favored affinal kinship over agnatic kinship (Herlihy 2004; Duby 2007). This kinship structure stressing affinity is still dominate in Bosnia-Herzegovina although no longer in Europe. Establishing close kinships through marriage is a cultural custom of not only Bosniaks, but also Croats and Serbs in Bosnia-Herzegovina. While members of different faith traditions (Catholicism, Orthodoxy, Islam), the large majority of Bosnians share this cultural heritage of strong affinal kinship which persevered from their early Middle Ages through Ottoman and Austro-Hungarian rule and into the modern era. This kinship custom does not come from the Ottoman Turks. It is not even shared as strongly with other South Slavs. The custom existed in the early Middle Ages in Europe, of which Bosnia was a part. The custom in Europe died out in the later Middle Ages as agnatic kin assumed greater importance and status. The custom, however, is immanent in Bosnia-Herzegovina, in part due to the need for society to live after the historical pogroms suffered in which agnatic kin were killed (Doubt and Tufekčić 2019; Doubt 2014). To speak culturally rather than sociopolitically or legally, Bosnia-Herzegovina reflects an image of Europe that Europe needs to see in order to see itself better. It is this image the Dayton Accords kills.

Chapter Five

Social Order without Scapegoating

A Critique of René Girard

Although people in Bosnia-Herzegovina adamantly insisted to outsiders that they were not scapegoats, journalistic accounts and politicians in the international community and the Balkans would treat people in Bosnia-Herzegovina as scapegoats. It is helpful to review the limits of this concept with respect to explaining and redressing the causes of sociocide.

The concept of scapegoating has widely used descriptive power with respect to reporting and understanding social violence. The disciplines of psychology, sociology, literary criticism, theology, and rhetoric each have particular versions of what scapegoating is as a social phenomenon. One reason the concept is confusing is because these multiple versions converge in scholarly discussions. While the different versions are not mutually exclusive, their mixing creates confusion. It is worthwhile to distinguish the different versions, review their interconnectedness, and critique the flaws in the dominate discussion of scapegoating found in the work of René Girard. We are concerned with the soul of society and with the erasing of the soul of society, and at the end of this chapter we will cite Martin Buber to dramatize this concern.

Scapegoating is biblical in its origins. A scapegoat is a sacrificial object, whether animal or human, through which a society purges itself of its sins. The transgressions of a society are first projected onto the scapegoat. A transference occurs. Then, the scapegoat is expelled and with it the transgressions of the community that were symbolically projected onto the scapegoat. A state of guiltlessness is established in the conscience of the society. Although society's conscience is cleared, society is not self-conscious about how it cleared its conscience.

On the surface, there is not a difference between being a victim and being a scapegoat. Both the victim and the scapegoat suffer. Both panic. Each dreads violence. Analytically, there is a difference. Unlike the victim, whose suffering may be either accidental or intentional, the scapegoat takes on symbolic significance. There is a ritual through which the scapegoat is labelled, objectified, and reified. The person scapegoated loses her or his voice and comes to represent something arbitrarily connected to who she or he is. The result is prejudice. The person being scapegoated becomes trapped in a ritual that has biblical nuances but inhuman consequences. Violence under the cloak of blinding righteousness follows.

In psychology, the idea of scapegoating is used to explain victimization in families. As a scapegoat, an individual is treated as an object against whom the prejudice of the group is projected. The individual becomes a lightning rod for the group's hatred, which, in fact, is a self-hatred even though it seems to be focused on another. Because the group, whether a family or a peer group, cannot live with this hatred of itself, it transfers its unwanted feeling unto another. The transference is perverse in that the group's self-hatred becomes entrenched. Co-optation of the victim is necessary. A vicious and seemingly unbreakable cycle is maintained, and the ritual is deepened.

In sociology, the idea of scapegoating is used to explain the way in which a community may attempt to establish order. The scapegoat is an object lesson. In order for members of a society to feel secure, they commit violence against one who has been singled out. The members of the society inflict on one of their own what they either consciously or unconsciously fear could be inflicted upon themselves. This anxiety triggers scapegoating, and its purpose is to relieve the group of its collective fear, leading to social tranquility.

René Girard is the most eloquent proponent of this theory. In *Violence and the Sacred*, Girard puts forth an account of scapegoating explicitly as a concept in literary criticism and implicitly as a sociological theory. Girard argues that scapegoating is necessary as well as inevitable in the history of societies. According to Girard, scapegoating is ritualized violence that, when done unanimously, stops violence and establishes social order. If scapegoating is done with the consent of the entire community (the lynchpin of his theorizing), it suppresses the possibility of reciprocity. "Unanimity is a formal requirement; the abstention of a single participant renders the sacrifice even worse than useless—it makes it dangerous" (1977, 100). The idea is analogous to the Hobbesian social contract. To establish social order, members of society unanimously agree to surrender their right to use force and fraud, either out of fear, innate rationality, or the persuasiveness of scapegoating.

As a prelude to his formulation of scapegoating, Girard articulates the state of nature called the "Hobbesian jungle":

The fear generated by the kill-or-be-killed syndrome, the tendency to "antici-pate" violence by lashing out first (akin to our contemporary concept of "pre-ventive war") cannot be explained in purely psychological terms. . . . In a universe both deprived of any transcendental code of justice and exposed to violence, everyone has reason to fear the worst. The difference between a projection of one's own paranoia and an objective evaluation of circumstances has been worn away. (1977, 54)

Girard and Hobbes have the similar understanding of the state of nature as violent, lawless, and chaotic. Note here that there is no transcendental code of justice. Fear is all powerful; reason totally absent; and objectivity com-pletely lost.

Girard's solution for evolving out of the Hobbesian jungle, however, is antithetical to Hobbes's solution. To understand Girard's account of scape-goating as a solution to the problem of social order, it is best first to review Hobbes's account. As explained earlier, the Hobbesian social contract repre-sents the birth of society. Society is created when a collection of people recognizes that life becomes peaceful when they collectively agree to sus-pend their use of force and fraud against each other and when this agreement is binding. Without this social contract, life always remains short, nasty, and brutish. Without the social contract, violence is necessary, and violence dom-inates. With this social contract, violence is viewed as unnecessary—neces-sarily unnecessary. For Hobbes, society is grounded in this cognitive con-struction, nothing more (Parsons 1968). H. L. A. Hart's theory of jurispru-dence is grounded in this same concept (Dworkin 1977, 16–39). Society is born when people collectively recognize the utilitarian rationality of the so-cial contract. The social contract is the more efficient means of attaining a peaceful and long life than each individuals' unchecked and simultaneous use of force and fraud.

What convinces people to accept the social contract? For Hobbes, the answer is empirical. The hellish experience of a war of all against all and our primal memory of this experience compels us to accept the rationality of the social contract. The history of social violence is the record of forgetting and re-remembering this lesson, the ebb and flow of irrational and rational con-duct. Society is the birth of the distinction between complying in deference to another's potential use of force or fraud and obeying out of respect for the legitimacy of the state and the innate rationality of the social contract. Au-thority is the notion that a group of people (a society) collectively accepts a rule as rationally binding. There is no transcendental code of justice here.

Girard has a strikingly anti-Hobbesian understanding of the solution to the problem of social order, which Girard and Hobbes both understand clear-ly. Girard's theorizing depicts the presocial nature of human nature more starkly than Hobbes, but his theorizing debunks the foundational ideas that the mainstream of sociology inherits from Hobbes. In Girard's work, natural right is not suspended, nor is it critiqued. Natural right is masked. It, in fact, is embedded in the very notion of social right. The idea that "might is right" is implicitly preserved in society's evolution. When society scapegoats, society is mightiful and therefore rightful. For Girard, social right is right simply because it is the most forceful, that is, a unanimous expression of natural right. The origins of society is its inherent lawlessness, which is ontologically no different than the state of nature. As Girard says, we live in "a universe deprived of any transcendental code of justice" (1977, 54). Scapegoating represents this fact for society.

Girard says violence is inevitable. It is true that in a state of nature violence is inevitable. Hobbes says, thanks to the social contract, violence is not inevitable. It is necessary, therefore, to understand why violence is not inevitable in society. Girard and Hobbes each address the role of envy in recounting the origins of society. Envy, they say, is an intrinsic feature of the human species. Human beings are social; one way in which that sociability is expressed is through envy. For Girard, envy is superior to rationality. Envy trumps rationality, which is why scapegoating rather than the social contract achieves social order. For Hobbes, rationality is superior to envy. If it were not, there would not be a society. Society would never rise above the state of nature. For Hobbes, rationality and envy work together, collude, to establish the social contract. The social contract is created not simply because of our rationality (the strict utilitarian understanding of social order) but also because of our capacity to put ourselves in the place of another. If we use violence against another, another will at some point use violence against us. Envy, which puts oneself in the place of another, is turned into a positive rather than a negative force. Since we do not want violence to be brought to bear against ourselves, we do not want violence to be brought to bear against another. Without rationality envy perpetuates violence. With rationality envy is transformed into empathy and compassion.

It therefore seems wrongheaded for Girard to argue that violence is imitable. To imitate, we must put ourselves in the place of the other. Our conscience must link ourselves to another. We must imagine and anticipate what and how another feels. We socially connect. When there is this identification with another, violence cannot occur. Violence cannot truly be imitated.

Violence, of course, can be copied, and in the state of nature, violence is copied. Revenge copycats the violent deed of another. Copying occurs without identification. Copying is a natural behavior; it is not a social one because it lacks identification with another. To say then that violence can be imitated is illogical; it places natural right, whether the natural right of a collective or the natural right of an individual, above social right. Social right must be grounded in trust. This trust is principled in that people imitate the rationality of the social contract in their social interactions.

Let us turn now away from sociology to theology. In theology, there is also a concept of scapegoating, and this version lurks in the background of secular discussions of the phenomenon. It is important to distinguish the version of scapegoating found in theology in order to separate it from the secular versions. In the theology of the Abrahamic faiths, Christianity, Judaism, and Islam, God does not allow Abraham to sacrifice his son. God provides a ram as a substitute. The ram, not Abraham's son, is the scapegoat. The parable shows God's relation to humanity. God will not accept human sacrifices. Scapegoating of human beings is taboo. We cannot scapegoat another. All human beings are created in God's image. Divine law becomes human law through Abraham.

This imperative informs not just faith communities but any community grounded in the principle of human rights. The dividing line between a barbaric society and a civilized society is the depth of a society's taboo against scapegoating. If the taboo is strong, there is social stability. If the taboo is feeble, there is anomie. Societies, in which the media and popular culture promote the scapegoating ritual, are barbaric, hardly societies at all. In such communities, the absence of a social contract is naively perceived as the ideal social situation. Absolute freedom reigns back to back with absolute terror. When societies use the scapegoating ritual to sustain order, human rights are nonexistent.

We have surveyed the concept of scapegoating in psychology, sociology, and theology. We have indicated how theology provides a counterversion to the concept of scapegoating found in psychology and sociology. In literature, there are stories that dramatize scapegoating. Interestingly, such stories are especially vivid in the literature from the Balkans. Consider, for example, the Nobel Prize winner Ivo Andrić's (1977) *The Bridge on the Drina*, in which there is at the beginning of the novel the gory impaling of Radisav. Radisav is a scapegoat in several senses within the novel. He is a scapegoat for the failure to complete the bequeathed bridge; he is an object lesson to the citizens of Višegrad who observe this gruesome killing; and he is a martyr within the Serbian community who idealize him as a Christ figure. This literary example of scapegoating is artful but morally confusing; it unclearly mixes the psychological, sociological, political, and theological aspects of the concept. Moreover, in every dramatic scene after this opening one, Andrić continues to employ the scapegoat figure to frame his narrative. The novel never develops from or transcends the scapegoating of Radisav, which remains the primary epiphany in the novel. Every vignette after this opening and powerful scene is, in fact, a regression. *The Bridge on the Drina*, in other words, is the opposite of a Bildungsroman; de-education rather than education is its theme.

To review, in the social sciences, scapegoating is a mechanism for expressing prejudice; in literary criticism, it is a symbolic mechanism for purging a community of dissonance and establishing solidarity within a seemingly functional community. Ironically, literary criticism's account is the more sociological. For the purging of the scapegoat to be functional, there must be identification as well as disidentification. The scapegoat is never a total stranger. The scapegoat is instead selected from within the community.

Let us now turn to the concept of scapegoating in the discipline of rhetoric because it helps synthesize the previous discussions. Kenneth Burke provides a nuanced account of what scapegoating is for the discipline of rhetoric through the notion of "vicarious atonement."

> As such, [the scapegoat] is profoundly consubstantial with those who, looking upon it as a chosen vessel, would ritualistically cleanse themselves by loading the burden of their own iniquities upon it. Thus the scapegoat represents the principle of division in that its persecutors would alienate from themselves to it their own uncleanlinesses. For one must remember that a scapegoat cannot be "curative" except insofar as it represents the iniquities of those who would be cured by attacking it. In representing *their* iniquities, it performs the role of vicarious atonement (that is, unification, or merger, granted to those who have alienated their iniquities upon it, and so may be purified through its suffering). (1969, 406)

To consider an example, in *Yugoslavia: Death of a Nation*, Laura Silber and Allan Little note this incident at the beginning of Slobodan Milošević's ascendancy to power: "The crowd roared, screaming for the arrest of the Albanian Party leader [Azem Vlasi]. Milosevic answered: 'I can't hear you, but we will arrest those responsible including those who have used the workers. In the name of the socialist people of Serbia I promise this'" (1996, 68). Silber and Little then note that Dušan Mitević, chief of Belgrade TV and confidant of Milošević, said that this was Milošević at his best.

What is it about Milošević's utterance that is so admirable for Mitević? Milošević says he will arrest those who deceive the people, who are plotting against Yugoslavia, and who have used the workers. It is Milošević, however, who, at this very moment, is deceiving the people, plotting against Yugoslavia, and using the workers. The way in which Milošević describes Vlasi is less a description of Vlasi and more a description of himself. Milošević makes Vlasi his scapegoat. By transferring to Vlasi the crimes against the state of which he himself is guilty, Milošević becomes something other than himself. Milošević's guilt in undermining the state of Yugoslavia is projected and then transferred to Vlasi, who was put on a show trial and imprisoned. At the same time, Milošević co-opts Vlasi's innocence; he assumes Vlasi's integrity as a faithful Yugoslav. Burke formulates this rhetorical use of scapegoating in the political realm as "vicarious atonement." By scapegoating Vlasi, Milošević vicariously atones himself.

Donald Trump engages in a similar practice artfully scapegoating his opponents. During the presidential debates with Hillary Clinton in 2016, Trump called Clinton the devil and said he would put her in jail if he were elected president. At his political rallies, his supporters repeated the refrain, "Lock her up." Embracing the spirit of the "lock her up" mob chants at his rallies, during the debate Trump said, "If I win I am going to instruct my attorney general to get a special prosecutor to look into your situation—there has never been so many lies and so much deception." The way in which Trump describes Clinton is less a description of Clinton and more a description of himself. Trump makes Clinton his scapegoat. By transferring to Clinton the guilt for lies and deception of which he himself is guilty, Trump becomes something other than himself. Trump's guilt is projected and then transferred to Clinton, turning the presidential debate into a show trial which might lead to Clinton's imprisonment. At the same time, Trump co-opts Clinton's innocence; he assumes Clinton's integrity as he erases it. Again, Burke formulates this rhetorical use of scapegoating in the political realm as "vicarious atonement." By scapegoating Clinton, Trump vicariously atones himself, which is a ritual Trump, like Milošević, repeatedly uses to maintain his political superiority.

During such public utterances, people identify with Milošević and Trump; that is, they identify with what they are doing, namely, scapegoating. Milošević and Trump's unchecked use of the scapegoating ritual make their power seem unassailable, not only to their people but also to the outside world. While the subjects and victims of the ritual changed, the ritual remained the same. Political leaders in other communities learn to copy the scapegoat ritual for the purpose of attaining and securing power. That is, communities who are scapegoated retaliate by scapegoating the members of the community that had scapegoated them.

Aleksa Djilas shares the following comment with Tom Butler:

> When our conversation turned to Milošević, Aleksa Djilas declaimed: "My position is unique in Belgrade: he's guilty, but don't extradite him!" He chuckled as he told me that Latinka Perović was "mad" at him for his stand. I asked what was wrong with handing such djubre ("trash") as Milošević over to the Hague. Here, the British educated Djilas shed his urbanity, spitting out his words in a manner that reminded me of his late father: "But that would make him into a scapegoat!" (Butler 2001)

Why oppose the arrest of Milošević if he is guilty of war crimes and crimes against humanity? On what basis does Djilas resist this imperative? Djilas suggests that Western leaders underestimate the political power of scapegoating. Djilas dreads its consequences because he directly witnessed how scapegoating was used in political discourse in Serbia and how Tito used scapegoating against his father Milovan Djilas in Communist Yugoslavia.

The comparable problem occurred during Trump's impeachment. When the House of Representative impeached Trump sending their charges for trial to the US Senate, it made Trump a scapegoat among his supporters and garnered him more political support with them.

Consider other parallels. Arresting Milošević in Belgrade and transferring him to the Hague divided Milošević from the Serbian people. Impeaching Trump divided Trump from the US government. Milošević represented the guilt of the Serbian people; that is, in the name of a Greater Serbia he initiated, planned, incited, and carried out genocide. Trump represented the very increasing irresponsibility of the government and its betrayal of the American people. The division that the Belgrade arrest created seemed to initiate a curative process. In offering up Milošević as a scapegoat, the Serbian nation gave some sort of reparation. In impeaching Trump, the US Congress also seemed to initiate a curative process. In offering up Trump as a scapegoat, the US Congress gave some sort of reparation. The Serbian people seemed to cleanse themselves of their iniquities. The US Congress seemed to cleanse itself of its complicity in poor government. The reparation, however, is unreal; as Burke says, it is vicarious, and this was Djilas's prophetic point.

Events at the Hague where Milošević stood trial proved Djilas right. Milošević's line of defense created a kind of media event at the trial; he claimed that he was the sacrificial goat for the period when NATO bombed Serbia and Kosovo in 1999. Before the Tribunal's judges, Milošević acted out the scapegoat role. Milošević constructed the evidence for his case on the spot, as it were. Milošević's individual responsibility for the injustices that he inflicted on so many people and communities remained unjudged in Serbia even though the crimes were reported and witnessed. Before the Serbian people, Milošević became not just a scapegoat, but a martyr, and the judicial process backfired. The same could be said for the show-trial and bungled, vindictive execution of Saddam Hussein. "The disorderly trial and execution of Saddam Hussein focused on a fragment of the dictator's crimes and amounted, in the end, to little more than political theater" (Dower 2010, 367).

Scapegoating can be used to explain the way in which a community attempts to establish solidarity, a meaningful sense of interdependence among the members of a community. In order for members to feel secure and interconnected, they ritualistically commit violence against others who have been singled out. Collectively, members of the society inflict on some of their own what they all either consciously or unconsciously fear could be inflicted upon them. The anxiety within the group triggers the need for scapegoating; the purpose is to relieve the group of its anxiety so as to establish a strong sense of solidarity.

The task now is to construct the repudiation of scapegoating, provide its antidote, and demonstrate how this antidote works. The writing of Émile

Durkheim, in contrast to Hobbes, suggests that the notion of human rights is grounded in something more than empirical experience. In his essay, "Individualism and the Intellectuals," which is a sociological critique of the scapegoating ritual during the Dreyfus affair in France, Durkheim writes, "And since each of us incarnates something of humanity, each individual consciousness contains something divine and thus finds itself marked with a character which renders it sacred and inviolable to others" (1973, 52). Since each individual is sacred and thus inviolable, scapegoating is taboo, necessarily taboo. Since each individual is inviolable, no individual and no community can accept the scapegoating of any individual. When one is persuaded by this principle, one recognizes that there is moral unity only when the state itself defends this conviction. Scapegoating can never become unanimous because no individual would ever consent to being scapegoated, and the person scapegoated must be selected from the community. Girard's theorizing is based on a surreal fiction, one that is not just irrational but antirational. What is, in fact, unanimous is the taboo against scapegoating, and this unanimity is empirical as well as metaphysical. Martin Buber captures this point for our study of sociocide when he writes, "If a culture ceases to be centered in the living and continually renewed relational event, then it hardens into the world of *It*, which the glowing deeds of solitary spirits only spasmodically break through" (1958, 54).

The problem of social order cannot be resolved without reference to human rights. According to Durkheim, the social contract serves the interests of the individual and society equally: "Not only is individualism distinct from anarchy; but is henceforth the only system of beliefs which can ensure the moral unity of the country" (1973, 50). How is it that individualism and the moral unity of the country are affirmed simultaneously? Durkheim argues that a state may never accept scapegoating as a way to establish order because, "There is no reason of State which can excuse an outrage against the person when the rights of the person are placed above the State" (1973, 46). Durkheim observed that when society "tolerates acts of sacrilege it abdicates any sway over men's minds" (1973, 53). The transgression of this principle of governance explains the spiral of violence in not only former-Yugoslavia, but also Israel's oppression of the Palestinians, Russia's suppression of Chechnya, France's colonization of Algeria, and the US occupation of Iraq. When a state "tolerates acts of sacrilege, it abdicates any sway over men's minds" (Durkheim 1973, 53). Anomie and violence are the result. To cite Buber again, "And in all the seriousness of truth, hear this: without *It* man cannot live. But he who lives with *It* alone is not a man" (1958, 34). In this context, without It society cannot live. But a society that lives with It alone is not a society. Think here of It as the empirical world.

Consider now Robert Hayden's discussion of the Dayton Accord in "Focus: Constitutionalism and Nationalism in the Balkans":

> The Dayton Constitution . . . gives priority to human rights. Yet these are
> meaningless. As James Madison notes in 1787, "In framing a government . . .
> the great difficulty lies in this: you must first enable the government to control
> the governed; and in the next place oblige it to control itself." (1995, 68)

While negative in content, Hayden's citation to Madison is revealing. How
does a government control the governed? One way in which the government
controls the governed is through the use of force and fraud. Madison, however, indicates that if all the government does is control the governed, no matter
how efficiently and effectively, it is not a government. Such a government
can only resort to increasingly sophisticated forms of force and fraud, and
this militarization of the police is the road to hell. The government itself is
out of control.

Madison says that the government is obliged to control itself. But what
obliges a government to control itself? There is only one way to oblige a
government to control itself: when it gives priority to human rights. Giving
priority to human rights is tantamount to the government controlling itself.
Giving priority to human rights obliges a government to control itself as it
controls the governed. The commitment to human rights wins the consent of
the governed to be governed by the government, to be governed by what
governs the government. The best, the most efficient, and so, ultimately, the
most rational way for a government to control the governed is to respect
human rights. In the next chapter, we digress and address the government's
use of torture after reviewing Max Weber's understanding of sociology as the
study of social action.

Chapter Six

The Reality of Torture and Sociocide

"Sociology (in the sense in which this highly ambiguous word is used here) is a science that attempts the interpretive understanding of social action in order thereby to arrive at a causal explanation of its course and effects" (1947, 88). Max Weber's definition of sociology is challenging. It presents a contradiction that is hard to ignore. Interpretive understanding does not arrive at causal explanations. Experimental research arrives at causal explanations. At best, interpretive understanding establishes correlations, which research methods students are taught. The methodology that Weber has sociology use to arrive at causal explanations is inadequate from the empirical point of view. Weber's definition of sociology puts sociology in a double-bind. Does sociology then change its goal or its methods?

Weber curses sociology with his definition, which accounts for sociology's institutionalized obsession with inferential statistics in order to compensate for this inadequacy. Quantitative sociologists can arrive at causal explanations or at least a simulation of causal explanations with inferential statistics and multivariate analysis. When we think about it, however, inferential statistics is itself a type of interpretive understanding, one that ritualizes a positivistic epistemology and handcuffs the true purpose of interpretive understanding in sociology. Weber points out, "If adequacy in respect to meaning is lacking, then no matter how high the degree of uniformity and how precisely its probability can be numerically determined, it is still an incomprehensive statistical probability, whether dealing with overt or subject processes" (1947, 99). With inferential statistics one may arrive at statistical significance tantamount to causal explanation but at the same time attain no sociological significance. Statistical significance and sociological significance stand on two different ontologies. This hegemonic focus on statistical significance in sociological inquiry diminishes the importance of interpretative understanding.

Just as numbers are the domain of mathematics, law the domain of jurisprudence, and politics the domain of political science, action is the domain of sociology. "Action is social in so far as, by virtue of the subjective meaning attached to it by the acting individual (or individuals), it takes account of the behavior of others and is thereby oriented in its course" (1947, 88). Here is how sociology is different from psychology. Sociology studies action and psychology studies behavior, whether it be animal behavior or human behavior. The difference between action and behavior, of course, is not always clear: "The line between meaningful action and merely reactive behavior to which no subjective meaning can be attached, cannot be sharply drawn" (1947, 90). Is human conduct meaningful action or merely reactive behavior? We cannot always tell, even for our own human conduct.

Weber also blesses sociology with his definition, a blessing he is proud to give, but which few sociologists fully appreciate. Interpretive understanding is the modus operandi of sociology. Weber stresses the importance of this point. "We can accomplish something which is never attainable in the natural sciences, namely the subjective understanding of the action of the component individuals. The natural sciences on the other hand cannot do this, being limited to the formulation of causal uniformities in objects and events and the explanation of individual facts by applying them" (1947, 103). Weber is joyful. He identifies the vocation of the discipline, its advantage vis-á-vis the natural sciences. Weber feels that what sociology accomplishes makes it superior to the natural sciences and superior as an empirical science. Few sociologists appreciate this blessing. When sociologists are addressing a subject sociologically, they are addressing it as social action. Such is the sociologist's frame of reference.

This chapter will now address torture as social action, focusing on the subjective meaning attached to it. Torture, of course, can be interpreted just as behavior rather than action. If a village captures a shot-down bomber crew, their brutality and cruelty toward the bomber crew may be a reactive behavior. Their behavior as a crowd is hot blooded.

Torture can also be interpreted as social action, a social action that has an end, a means, a motive, and a normative orientation. The normative orientation links the different aspects of action (Parsons 1968). An example of a normative orientation would be to love to work. An opposing one would be to work to love. Another example of a normative orientation would be to eat to live. An opposing one would be to live to eat. These normative orientations, their differences, produce different actions. The normative orientation is what is missing in the interpretation of human conduct as behavior. We can understand behavior perfectly well without understanding its normative orientation or needing to assume it even has a normative orientation. However, once we understand behavior as having a normative orientation, we no longer understand it as behavior but as action.

The means the torturer uses as an actor is prolonged and systematic pain to the human being being tortured. A former Guantanamo prisoner reported he was beaten, stripped naked, subjected to intimidation by dogs, hooded, thrown against a wall, and sustained electric shocks from a generator. He reported he endured sexual humiliation where "a naked woman entered the interrogation room and smeared him with what he believed to be menstrual blood." Another Guantanamo prisoner reported he was forced to lie down in urine and sodomized with a broomstick.

The motive of this action is to make the person being tortured talk, "to force from *one* tongue . . . the secrets of everything" (Sartre 2006, xix). The assumption underlying this motive is described by Jean-Paul Sartre: "Whispered propaganda would have us believe that 'everybody talks,' and this ignorance of humanity excuses torture. As everyone of us is a potential traitor, the killer in each of us need feel no qualms. All the more so, as the honeyed voices tell us every day that the glory of France demands it" (Sartre 2006, xxxix). What is this ignorance of humanity reflected in torture? The ignorance is that humans are all base. There is a killer in each one of us. The torturer is no different than the one being tortured. The torturer simply has the advantage of having the power and opportunity to torture, and the person being tortured does not. The tacit assumption is that if the human being being tortured had the power and opportunity to torture, that human being being tortured would then torture the torturer. The torturer need not feel any guilt. The torturer, in fact, should feel proud. The glory of France demands this action. Torture protects one's country from one's enemies. It saves lives. A country must be strong enough to use this means if it wants to survive and not be destroyed by its enemies. The end justifies the means. "It is right to torture a man if his confession can save a hundred lives."

Torture can be carried out by a rogue subculture of fighters who are acting against the moral sentiments of their country that legally oppose the use of torture with captured prisoners. Think of the pictures of the US Reservist Lynndie England holding an Iraq prisoner on a leash and forcing him to crawl and another where England is pointing her finger at a naked Iraq prisoner who is hooded while he is forced to masturbate. A military court later convicted England on four counts of maltreating detainees and one count of committing an indecent act. This military action and sentencing frames her action as part of a rogue subculture and not representative of the country's moral principles. After serving her sentence, England, though, was unrepentant and said in a media interview, "They're trying to kill us, and you want me to apologize to them? It's like saying sorry to the enemy" (Estes 2012). England and her rogue subculture see the moral principles of the country opposed to the use of torture against captured prisoners as high minded and idealistic.

These principles, however, reflect not only moral reason, but also practical reason. While opposing France's extensive use of torture in Algeria in the sixties (a tactic that became a model for the US military in its global war on terror), Pierre-Henri Simon argued that "If really we are capable of a moral reflex which our adversary has not, this is the best justification for our cause, and even for our victory" (cited in Horne 2006, 205). A country's morale remains strong when it is convinced it possesses a moral reflex its adversary does not. This morale empowers the military and eventually leads it to victory. Soldiers are confident in what they are fighting for and in themselves.

General Colin Powell made a comparable argument. As Secretary of State, he wrote to the White House in January 2002, "A determination that Geneva does not apply could undermine U.S. military culture which emphasizes maintaining the highest standards of conduct in combat, and could introduce an element of uncertainty in the status of adversaries" (cited in Rowley and McGovern 2008). Simon and Powell's positions parallel each other. The laws of war require that military forces respect the Geneva conventions which absolutely prohibit torture and other cruel or inhuman treatment and outrages upon individual dignity. As Powell indicates, this respect is good for the military and ultimately protects the army. As the historical example of France in Algeria shows, when a country uses torture to fight an adversary, it may win the battle tactically but it loses the war strategically.

In an easily available essay titled, "The Case for Torture," Michael Levin (1982) argues that "The most powerful argument against the use of torture as a punishment or to secure confessions is that such practices disregard the rights of the individual." Levin is half right. What empowers the morale of the military to which Powell refers and what makes them a strong fighting force is its conviction that it possesses a moral reflex their adversary does not. Regard for the rights of the individual who is held as a prisoner is the moral reflex of which Simon speaks. When the military force respects this moral principle, it empowers the military and makes it a stronger fighting force. Here is the other half of Levin's argument, which he leaves out: The military's respect for the individual human rights of captured prisoners who are the enemy make it a powerful military force. This argument, both sides of it, is the best argument against torture because it is idealistic as well as pragmatic. The idealism is exemplified in its pragmatism, and the pragmatism is embodied in its idealism.

This point is essential when trying to heal the moral wounds of US soldiers who served in Iraq. "Guilt and shame can tear a self into pieces, to the point that one loses sound judgement about who one is and who one can be. The task is to recover lost goodness, to renew a desire to live well, and to find meaning" (Sherman 2015, 161). Nancy Sherman's *Afterwar: Healing the*

Moral Wounds of Our Soldiers examines how this process occurs and why it is essential.

Under the leadership of President Bush and Vice President Dick Cheney and the advice of Dick Cheney's lawyer, David Addington, and the White House Counsel Alberto Gonzales, the White House dismissed Powell's argument. At this point, torture no longer was the actions of a rogue subculture acting against the moral and legal principles of their country. Torture was institutionalized. This US leadership institutionalized torture. President Bush asserted that the Geneva Conventions did not apply to the United States' conflict with al Qaeda because al Qaeda was not a party to the Geneva Conventions. Afghanistan, however, was a party to the Geneva Conventions as was the United States. After the September 11 attacks, the White House constituted a rogue subculture vis-á-vis the global community that was party to the Geneva Conventions. When President Obama, despite his campaign promises, chose not to investigate the previous administration for war crimes, letting bygones be bygones and looking forward rather than backward, he tacitly preserved Bush's legacy. President Trump has come to embrace this legacy in an open and brazen way. The detention center at Guantánamo Bay, Cuba, where torture has been occuring (first opened in 2002) has not been closed despite President Obama's promises to do so. Within the country of the United States, the White House no longer was a rogue subculture; it institutionalized a political policy that endorsed the use of torture against captured prisoners.

The slogan Global War on Terrorism used after the September 11th attacks is misleading. Terrorism is not an enemy. Terrorism is a method. The enemies of the United States use terrorism as a method. At the same time, the allies of the United States use terrorism as a method. Moreover, the United States uses terrorism as a method. Torture is a terroristic method. Levin is right when he says the purpose of torture is not to punish captured prisoners. Punishment occurs in a legal system, whether legal-rational or tribal; it requires a trial, a judgment, and a sentence. Torture is not even revenge except when viewed as behavior, for example, when a village captures a shot-down bomber crew and inflicts its brutality and cruelty toward the captured bomber crew. Even the waterboarding of Khalid Sheikh Mohammed, who was named as the chief architect of the 9/11 attacks, 183 times is not revenge, although it certainly looks like revenge. The method of torture is to terrorize. The terror is viewed as an "ideal truth pill" (Žižek 2008, 43). Torture's purpose is simply terror.

Torture reflects a victor's justice, where, as Sartre says, the torturer wants "to convince themselves and their victims of their invincible power" (Sartre 2006, xxxii). Here is the belief behind the victor's justice: First, it is better to do wrong than suffer wrong and, second, it is worse to suffer wrong than to do wrong. When wrong is used to fight wrong, that wrong becomes itself good. Torture operationalizes this very powerful cultural belief. The victor's justice lacks the moral reflex of which Simon spoke and which Simon argued was imperative not to lose.

The consequence of torture as action is "to make the prisoner feel like they do not belong to the same species" (Sartre 2006, xxxii). Slavoj Žižek (2008, 45) formulates this point in a telltale way when he says that torture is the abolition of the dimension of the neighbor. The first great commandment that Jesus gave his followers was "Love the Lord your God with all your heart and with all your soul and with all your mind." The second great commandment was "Love thy neighbor as thyself." Jesus said all the law and prophets depend upon these two laws. Žižek is asserting that the function of torture is to abolish the second commandment because the tortured subject is no longer a neighbor.

Another way to make this point is that the enemy is someone whose story you have not heard (Žižek 2000). Torturers do not hear their enemies, do not hear their enemies' stories, no matter how much the enemy being tortured talks. Here is why torture persists seemingly endlessly with no stop. Speaking of the torturers, Alleg says, "But no, their heads are empty and their work keeps them too busy and then they only half-believe in what they are doing" (Sartre 2006, xliii). While being tortured, Alleg persisted in telling his story to his torturers and reminding his torturers that he was their neighbor. If a story from the enemy is heard, torture stops because the tortured subject now is a neighbor, a member of the same species. The enemy is a neighbor, someone to whom you can say I am sorry. The second great commandment comes into play. As Žižek indicates, torture is the abolition of the second great commandment, the cornerstone of Christianity, as a guiding normative orientation in social action for society.

Torture is sociocidal, and it is important to address why and how. In *A Savage War for Peace: Algeria 1954–1962,* Alistair Horne asserts that "torture ends up corrupting the torturer as much as it breaks the victim" (2006, 200–201). Torture is sociocidal not because of the harm it does to the person who is tortured but because of the harm it does to the person who is doing the torture. This harm seeps into the torturer's community. Žižek extends this critical point that Horne makes about the war in Algeria to the United States' Global War on Terrorism.

> Abu Ghraib was not simply a case of American arrogance towards a Third World people: in being submitted to humiliating tortures, the Iraqi prisoners were effectively *initiated into American culture.* They were given a taste of its obscene underside, which forms the necessary supplement to the public values of personal dignity, democracy, and freedom. Bush was thus wrong: what we are getting when we see the photos of the humiliated Iraqi prisoners on our screens and front pages is precisely a direct insight into American values, into

the very core of the obscene enjoyment that sustains the U.S. way of life. (2008, 176)

Some might argue that there is no evidence for this assertion and it is simply anti-American. There, though, is evidence for the assertion—clear and direct evidence of how torture insidiously pervades American culture making its culture toxic and nihilistic. Torture porn is a common element in American cinema and television (Edelstein 2006). Thriller movies feature protracted torture scenes which become the climax of the film. Mel Gibson's "The Passion of Christ" treats the story of Jesus' crucifixion as a long, protracted pagan torture ritual, where Christ suffers repeated beatings and slashings, corporal cruelty for twelve hours. Without citing too many examples ("Hostel," "The Devil Rejects," "Saw," "Wolf Creek," "Make Them Die Slowly"), the function of modern cinema use of torture scenes is a radical moral displacement. The function is to make torture normative, to give torture the power of the normative.

Not only do the films depict torture, but they torture viewers with their unimaginable and unanticipated cruelty, forcing viewers to become mesmerized consumers of torture porn. When the military tortured Iraqi prisoners, it introduced Iraqi prisoners to the obscene underside of American culture, an inheritance of the military. For this reason, torture ends up corrupting the torturer as much as it breaks the victim. Horne's point can be extended from an interpersonal interaction to the societal level. When a country institutionalizes the use of torture against captured enemies who may or may not have used terrorism as a political method, it corrupts the country, forcing it either unconsciously and consciously to fall into nihilism's embrace. Here is why torture is sociocidal: Torture ends up corrupting the torturer and torturer's country not only as much as but far more than the person being tortured.

Chapter Seven

The Lure of the Pariah

Hannah Arendt, W. E. B. DuBois, and Franz Fanon

The identity of the pariah is an intelligible and compelling moral commitment after having had the experience of being scapegoated or tortured. The concept of the pariah helps us understand human identity in the face of the sociocidal forces of war and violence. In this chapter, the logic of the identity from within the logic itself is first provided. Then, drawing upon exoteric moral principles, a critical account of the pariah's logic is offered.

Given the experience of endless injustices, the pariah makes a decision. While the community that abuses the pariah views the pariah as a scapegoat, the pariah rejects this label. The pariah instead chooses to make the history of suffering, what the pariah inherits but does not choose, a necessary feature of one's identity. Victimization is turned into a resource, the foundation for self-formation and self-affirmation over which the pariah has autonomy and ultimate authority. One's individual and one's collective trauma are opportunities to empower oneself and discover one's authentic human identity.

The pariah opposes the unjust society as a rebel. Franz Fanon provides a way to explain this necessarily violent rebellion: "Decolonization is quite simply the substitution of one 'species' of mankind by another" (1968, 35). In this formulation, there is no universal human species of humanity, which Karl Marx (2004, 34) refers to as "the present, living species, as a *universal* and consequently free being." There instead is one particular human species being pitted against another, each asserting itself as superior and at the same time each asserting the non-importance and insignificance of the other. The principle of "a *universal* and consequently free being" is jettisoned. For the pariah, the call to transcend the boundaries of race, gender, nationality, or ethnicity for the principle of a transcendent notion of humanity is simply a trap; political freedom in a prejudiced society is an illusion; and assimilation in the settler's hegemonic culture is a ruse.

For the pariah, the goal cannot be to educate an oppressive society to make it a truly just society. Audre Lorde objects to this task assigned to her for a feminist conference, a white, bourgeoise, feminist conference. Conference organizers assigned her the responsibility to educate them about women of color and women on the margins. Lorde said the assigned task simply perpetuates oppression and racism under the pretense of openness and false generosity. "This is an old and primary tool of all oppressors to keep the oppressed occupied with the master's concerns. Now we hear that it is the task of women of color to educate white women—in the face of tremendous resistance—as to our existence, our differences, our relative roles in our joint survival. This is a diversion of energies and a tragic repetition of racist patriarchal thought" (1984, 102). The essential goal instead is to claim what is unique about oneself as a human vis-á-vis the dehumanizing social order of the powerful. Taking on the assigned responsibilities of the oppressor sabotages one's ability to undertake this compelling task.

Hannah Arendt (1944) develops the concept of the pariah as a profound and deep human commitment in an unjust and racist political order. She admires the intelligence, reflectiveness, and cleverness of the pariah. The pariah has an insider and outsider view of social order. The only understanding worthy of respect for the pariah is the understanding of one's own self and soul. The pariah thus devalues the call to understand the collective soul of humanity. It is a vain and futile effort, according to the pariah's logic and experience.

Fanon speaks against the naivete of the European educated Algerian intellectual who seeks to bridge the conflicted cultures of the colonizer and the colonized with a joint communique from a transcendent standpoint. Fanon advises this intellectual to abandon such a path and sever all relations to the European settler. The colonized intellectual, Fanon says, must make a choice. Is she French or is she Algerian? Is he French or is he Algerian? One cannot be both. An authentic life is found only by locating oneself exclusively within the dignity of one's own people.

To give a telltale example from the Balkans, when Mihailo Marković (Secor 1999) transforms himself from a Marxist Praxis philosopher in the sixties to a Belgrade Serbian nationalist in the eighties, he follows Fanon's advice. In the sixties and seventies, Marković was a world-renowned critical theorist for his writing on Marxism, humanism, social democracy, and human rights. Marković was a leading member of the editorial board of *Praxis* and the Korcula Summer School Board. Praxis is a humanistic, nonmetaphysical reformulation of what Marx meant by the notion of the human species-being in his writing on modern alienation. Praxis is emancipated, social, human activity. Praxis is the fuel and the product of a healthy society.

Marković published widely. He has essays in many anthologies. There are scholarly, academic books that focus extensively on Marković's work, for example, Gerson S. Sher's *Praxis: Marxist Criticism and Dissent in Socialist Yugoslavia* (1977).

In 1975, the Serbian Parliament brought charges of political deviance against Marković and seven other academicians, and they were removed from their university positions on charges of corrupting the youth. *Praxis* was banned, and the group became known as the Belgrade 8. Protests from American professors such as Noam Chomsky, Daniel Bell, and Stanley Hoffman did not change the Yugoslav government's decision (Secor 1999).

What became morally vexatious was that Marković, known among admiring leftists for both his humanistic critique of oppressive political practices and then his political persecution in Serbia for taking this stand, became a major supporter of Slobodan Milošević. Marković became, not a passive spectator, but a significant player on behalf of Milošević's rise to power. Marković helped navigate the Serbian people in Yugoslavia into the jaws of nationalism. The role that Marković played on behalf of Milošević's Belgrade regime in its acts of genocide and crimes against humanity must not be understated. He was a key ideologue for Milošević. Magas writes:

> This unexpected, indeed astonishing, alignment of *Praxis* editors with nationalism has aroused considerable dismay among their friends and sympathizers, for it delineates a complete break with the political and philosophical tradition represented by the journal. (1993, 52)

Marković chose to become a pariah and jettison his esteemed history in the tradition of critical theory.

On the surface, the pariah's consciousness is similar to what W. E. B. DuBois (2016) speaks of as double-consciousness. In the early 1900s, DuBois said that the Negro in America is gifted with a second sightedness, seeing American society through black eyes as well as through white eyes. For this reason, the African American possesses a deeper understanding of not only his soul but also America's soul. The African American, DuBois said, can be both African and American. Being African does not exclude being American. Being American does not exclude being African. The African American merges both identities not only for his or her sake but also for America's sake and its higher purpose as a nation. DuBois saw African Americans playing the primary role in the preservation of what is morally good about America. DuBois' advice to African Americans is a counterpoint to Fanon's advice to the colonized intellectual in Algeria.

While Arendt admires the intelligence, reflectiveness, and cleverness of the pariah, she argues that, despite its depth, the pariah's thinking is flawed. The fate of the intellectual who seeks to transcend racial, gender, national, or ethnic boundaries through a universal principle is treacherous, but the fate of the pariah is far worse. The fate of the pariah is self-annihilation. The thinking of the pariah eventually divorces itself from the distinction between right and wrong as witnessed in Marković's political transformation. Moral reasoning becomes brutish. The barbarian's viewpoint rules. The distinction between right and wrong is fundamental to the dignity of the pariah's people, but the distinction between right and wrong does not itself originate within the pariah's people. The distinction between right and wrong and the principle of human dignity are part of a larger whole, a collective humanity that transcends national boundaries.

Fanon as well recognizes this truism; he himself cannot sustain an absolute commitment to the pariah's position. Consider a statement that Fanon (1968, 199) later makes to conclude a chapter in *The Wretched of the Earth*:

> The building of a nation is of necessity accompanied by the discovery and encouragement of universalizing values. . . . It is at the heart of national consciousness that international consciousness lives and grows. And this two-fold emerging is ultimately only the source of all culture.

With his own moral reasoning Fanon reflectively refutes his earlier position.

Every ethnic and racial community that has suffered egregious injustices is drawn to the pariah's logic. Within the Balkans, the Serbian people after suffering greatly during World War II under the control of Nazi Germany embraced the pariah's position perhaps more passionately than other ethnic groups, which is not to say other ethnic groups did not also suffer greatly. The theology of Justin Popović and the Serbian Orthodox Church are strong influences in this regard. Because the experience of suffering grants the exclusive authority with which to speak about suffering, only the pariah has the authority with which to tell the pariah's story. The experience of the pariah tyrannically controls the narrative. The pariah rejects philosophy, which would challenge the exclusive privilege of experience to speak for itself. The pariah's story becomes solipsistic. Meaningful discourse with others is rejected; dialogue and conversation are impossible. Alan Blum (1992, 80) explains the problem: "The limits of the pariah are shown in the fact that his desire to write the history of suffering conflicts with his rejection of discourse. The pariah rejects discourse because discourse undermines the authority of fraternity and puts into question the privileged authority of the sufferer himself by making him account for the claim to privileged authority of his experience." The suffering of the pariah's people becomes incommunicable except to those who lived through this same experience. There is no invitation to read the history of suffering the pariah writes.

Svetosavlje is the word that the Serbian religious community uses to speak of the positive, enlightened side of Serbian nationalism. One principle of *svetosavlje* is that there can be no happiness for individuals themselves without the happiness of the people to which they belong (Lukić 2001). *Svetosavlje* represents what Durkheim (2003) would call mechanical solidarity in contrast to organic solidarity. With mechanical solidarity, the substance of the collective determines the character of the individual. One typical example offered is the Amish community: the Amish tradition essentially determines the social character of the individual in the community. The same sense of interdependency between an ethnic community and its members is the principle of nationalism.

With organic solidarity, it is the opposite; the substance of the individual determines the character of the collective. The more refined and sophisticated the specificity of an individual's occupation, the more developed and civilized the society itself. This type of solidarity arises from what Durkheim calls the division of labor. The solidarity of Yugoslav society had been more organic than mechanical. The distinctive culture of its ethnic communities did not detract from the solidarity of the whole. The distinctive character of different ethnic groups contributed to the wholistic character and vibrant nature of the society itself. There was unity in difference. Bosnia, as Ivo Banac indicated earlier, was an authentic representation of this type of social solidarity and Yugoslavia its formal imitation. One way to characterize "ethnic cleansing" in post-Communist Yugoslavia is to say that it represented a concerted effort on the part of ethno-nationalist politicians to transform the organic solidarity of Yugoslav society into the mechanical solidarity of a particular national ethnic group. To achieve this goal and develop nation-states founded on a romanticized sense of mechanical solidarity of one particular ethnic group, not only the nation of Yugoslavia but also the society of Bosnia-Herzegovina had to be killed.

A mechanistic society is one in which the community comes before the individual. As Durkheim (2003, 40) says, "at the moment when this solidarity exercises its force, our personality vanishes, as our definition permits us to say, for we are no longer ourselves, but the collective life." Herein lies the principle for the theological notion of *svetosavlje* (Lukić 2001). What holds together the Serbian people for nationalists is the mechanical solidarity of the people as a community.

Is *svetosavlje* a positive example of what Durkheim means by mechanical solidarity? The answer is yes and no. What holds the Serbian people together is the solidarity of the nation over the solidarity of people as individuals according to nationalists. The Serbian Orthodox Church is the guardian and guarantor of this solidarity, even more so than the Serbian government which is deferent to its higher religious authority so as to stay in power. The conflation between the state and the church is called philetism.

There is a problem, however. Serbian nationalism also represents a negative solidarity in that it has been established through war crimes, crimes

against humanity, and genocide. Negative solidarity does not produce integration by itself. Negative solidarity is grounded in hate. The Serbian philosopher, Radomir Konstantinović, in his untranslated work titled *Filosophija
palanka* [*Provincial Philosophy*] describes the problem.

> The entire Serbian Romanticism, especially in its final period, is imbued with
> the fear of man outside the kin . . . inspired by the fear of the non-kindred man
> as a monster: to the Romanticist in this culture man can be either a Serb or a
> monster (Konstantinović cited in Anzulovic 1999, 80).

The theology of the Serbian Orthodox Church reflects what Konstantinović
calls Serbian Romanticism. The more the Serbian Orthodox Church defines
the Serbian nation through negative relation to others, whether these mon-
sters are the Pope, Catholics, Europeans, humanists, Martin Luther, Muslims,
or Albanians, the less the integrity of Christian faith integrates the Serbian
community.

   Notice the paradox. Negative solidarity does not produce integration by
itself because there is nothing specific about it. Insofar as the Serbian Orthodox Church defines itself in a solipsistic manner, independently of civiliza-
tion and Christianity, the Serbian Orthodox Church has nothing specific
about its self, despite the multiplicity of specificities that are integral to its
historical integrity and faith tradition. In having no positive relation to what
is not itself, in not having a connection in a self-conscious and positive way
to what it is not itself, the Serbian Orthodox Church cannot have an authentic
relation to itself. The specificity the Serbian Orthodox Church claims for
itself becomes insubstantial insofar as the specificity is expressed through
antipathy toward what is other than itself. Mirko Đorđević (1996, 30) explains the implications of this solipsism.

> The Serbian Orthodox Church is undergoing one of the most difficult periods
> in its long history. Incapable of sowing the seeds of real Christianity, it has
> tilled the worst of its inheritance. Although overflowing with spiritual culture,
> its dogmatic precepts have brought it into conflict with the flow of current
> civilization. The spirit of salvation which brought the Christian church into the
> world in the first place has been replaced by the ideology of nationalism. . . .
> Ecumenicalism is, at best, understood as unnecessary "church diplomacy" and
> at worst, in the Justinian tradition, as a "mortal danger for the heavenly ark of
> our Church."

To create a pseudo-sense of mechanical solidarity qua nationalism, the Serbian Orthodox Church used the scapegoat ritual. Since scapegoating, however, is inherently negative in its consequences, scapegoating cannot itself posi-
tively integrate a community.

Consider the contemporary Serbian film, *Optimisti*, by Goran Paskaljević. The film depicts the madness of the pariah's sensibility. The film sublimely narrates the consequence of the divorce of the distinction between right and wrong from everyday social life. Each vignette in the film is the same; one striking vignette after another is a failed love story. The pariah's community suffers not only from a loss of confidence in moral reasoning, but also from an incapacity to love. Paskaljević shows a profound empathy toward the pathology of lovelessness. His aesthetic love, however, remains nontransformative. Nothing changes; nihilism is the sole faith.

Does the pariah live well? Is the soul of the pariah all that a human soul can be? Arendt concludes her account of the pariah with these twin statements: First, she says, regarding the individual, "For only within the framework of a people can a man live as a man among men, without exhausting himself" (1944, 122). This point is just as true for communities and nations: "And only when a people lives and functions in consort with other peoples can it contribute to the establishment upon earth of a commonly conditioned and commonly controlled humanity" (1944, 122). Arendt extends her point for individuals to nations.

The Palestinian poet Mahmoud Darwish comes from a Palestinian community cruelly abused and unjustly treated. Darwish, though, is not a pariah. He is a world poet. Darwish speaks of his love for an Israeli woman during his youth. It was formative for his soul, his worldview, his understanding of Israel, and his writing. The poetry of Darwish is not outsider art; it is insider art, all too sane and all too human. Darwish is a thoughtful sufferer, seeking to understand not his own but humanity's soul. His poetry grasps both. The following is a frequently cited stanza from Darwish's poetry: "Nothing is harder on the soul, than the smell of dreams, while they're evaporating."

In *Justice for Hedgehogs*, Ronald Dworkin (2013, 419–420) writes, "The two ethical ideals—living well and having a good life—are different. We can live well without having a good life: we may suffer bad luck or great poverty or serious injustice or a terrible disease and a premature death . . . we must each do what we can to make our own life as good as it could have been. You live badly if you do not try hard enough to make your life good." Here is the distinction that Foucault, adamantly and venomously spurns as we saw in the previous chapter. Consider the story in the contemporary Bosnian film, *Grbavica*. The mother was planning to attend medical school. During the war, she was raped by a Serbian soldier, who she calls a Chetnik, and had a child, a daughter, from the war as a consequence of being raped. She works late as a waitress in a nightclub. Her rich relatives do not help her. Still, she chooses to try to have a good life. She chooses to love her daughter despite her rage toward what her child reminds her of, and at the end of the film this choice gives her a good life. The thoughtful sufferer has a good life independently of being able to live well.

The politics in the United States is now embedded in the pariah's logic. Nationalism in the United States is influenced by a religious right and embraces the pariah's reasoning no less passionately than other nationalist communities. In *America Right or Wrong*, Anatol Lievan (2012, 18) asks intellectuals in the United States to do what is difficult for them, given how they, too, are seduced by the notions of American exceptionalism: "This book . . . is an appeal to American intellectuals to do what they have asked of intellectuals in other countries: to recognize and confront their own nationalism and to transcend it in the name of higher universal values." We will take up this charge concertedly in the next chapter.

Chapter Eight

The Spirit of Capitalism in the Face of the Coronavirus Pandemic

This study has focused on the ways in which the consequence of wars is sociocide. Other things than war may lead to sociocide. Disease may. The extinction of the Beothuks or Red Indians in Newfoundland, Canada, in the 1800s was due to disease. While some English routinely murdered the native population, putting a bounty on their heads, their extinction was due to tuberculosis contracted when the English interacted with the Beothuks. In 1768, the Beothuk population was 345; in 1811, 72; and in 1823, 11 or 12 (Marshall 1997, 444). Not having the immunity to fight the illness brought to the island from Europe, every Beothuk died. The material culture from the Beothuk community remains on the island, and it is the subject of local literature and archeological research.

The coronavirus pandemic threatens society globally. Moreover, the coronavirus throws a blinding light on the inequalities that undergird society. In the United States, the pandemic disproportionately impacts the poor, the elderly, prisoners, native Americans, and black Americans. Workers risk their lives, their own as well as their families, without sick leave or health insurance, for the benefit of the affluent. More than twenty million Americans are now unemployed with no wages or savings to live on. The Navajo Nation has the worst coronavirus cases per capita in the United States. In the state of Georgia, 80 percent of the deaths due to the coronavirus are black Americans, when black Americans constitute less than a third of the State of Georgia's population. Structural racism accounts for why this death rate is four to six times higher for black Americans. The pandemic lays bare the classism and racism that inhabits and structures the society of the United States, which privileged Americans prefer to deny. Will the pandemic mean that social, educational, moral, and spiritual responsibilities take precedence vis-á-vis financial responsibilities which, in a capitalist economy, are barbarically conceived (Banerjee and Duflo 2019)? Will the pandemic's exposure of grotesque injustices lead to progressive actions on the part of the government that protect and respect the needs and rights of all people? Will the pandemic's reality in all its concreteness and painfulness be persuasive in ways that moral arguments are not?

Karl Marx, Emile Durkheim, and Max Weber were each afraid of capitalism. The possibility that capitalism would kill society vexed their theorizing. Their sociologies reflected this fear. The promise of their sociologies was to ameliorate their fear. It behooves us at this time to revisit their theorizing.

Of sociology's three patriarchs, Marx was the least afraid of capitalism. During the French Revolution, the bourgeoise had been a revolutionary force. After overthrowing the aristocracy, the bourgeoise became the dominate class. The bourgeoise killed one society and replaced it with another. Notice that revolution is a kind of sociocide. Revolution kills one society in order to replace it with another and, hopefully, better society. The bourgeoise revolution brought a principle of legal equality, an end to feudal laws, and a philosophy of individual human rights.

According to Marx, the proletariat will overthrow the bourgeoisie much as the bourgeoise overthrew the aristocracy. The success of the bourgeoise society and its dependence upon capitalism mean its demise. As capitalism becomes stronger, capitalism sows the seeds of its own destruction. When capitalism assumes its pure form, it is not able to sustain itself. Marx (1977, 48) is poignant on this point.

> And here it becomes evident, that the bourgeoisie is unfit any longer to be the ruling class in society, and to impose its conditions of existence upon society as an over-riding law. It is unfit to rule because it is incompetent to assure an existence to its slave within his slavery, because it cannot help letting him sink into such a state, that it has to feed him, instead of being fed by him. Society can no longer live under this bourgeoisie, in other words, its existence is no longer compatible with society.

Marx anticipated that the proletarian revolution will lead to a better society just as the bourgeoise revolution led to a better society. "Just as, therefore, at an earlier period, a section of the nobility went over to the bourgeoisie, so now a portion of the bourgeoisie goes over to the proletariat" (Marx 1977, 46). Marx's attitude toward capitalism was "bring it on." Revolutions replace one society with another and hopefully better society.

The pandemic brings to the forefront the reckless and irresponsible failures of capitalistically motivated leaders. Without a viable and equitable health system for all (which American culture pejoratively refers to as social medicine), many are dying and will continue to die due to the pandemic. Millions have become unemployed with no income to pay for food or support families. Many are dying because they had to go to work, especially in public sector and health care jobs. Some in the US government want to end stay-at-home orders in order to open up the economy and sacrifice lives to do so. The inequality between those working in the public domain and those working safely at home will reach a breaking point. The pandemic throws a bright light on the social failure of capitalism. The capitalist society causes profound resentments within the society.

Durkheim was more afraid of capitalism than Marx. Durkheim saw capitalism, not leading to a different society, but destroying society. This fear is found in the concept of anomie. Capitalism degrades society to a society-less jungle. "We repeatedly insist in the course of this book upon the state of juridical and moral anomie in which economic life actually is found" (Durkheim 1933, 1). Education, government, science, public services, prisons, and even religious institutions become as normless as the economic life of free-market capitalism. Economic life comes to play an exclusive, dominate role, and social life is "only feebly ruled by morality" (Durkheim 1933, 2). Durkheim feared this anomie. When Americans refuse to wear masks and do social distancing in public spaces during the pandemic, they exemplify this lack of moral regulation. Durkheim also feared judicial anomie. When Senate Majority Leader Mitch McConnell nominates incompetent judges and President Trump appoints them to the bench, they insure judicial anomie.

Durheim (1933, 2) dreaded this de-evolution: "The most blameworthy acts are so often absolved by success that the boundary between what is permitted and what is prohibited, what is just and what is unjust, has nothing fixed about it, but seems susceptible to almost arbitrary change by individuals." Let us return to war, which is the primary subject of this study. The more anomic society, the more war—as the most profitable endeavor of the military industrial complex—flourishes. US President Dwight D. Eisenhower (1961) expressed a fear of the developing military-industrial complex and its influence on society: "We have been compelled to create a permanent armaments industry of vast proportions. Added to this, three and a half million men and women are directly engaged in the defense establishment. We annually spend on military security alone more than the net income of all United States corporations." The combination of war and capitalism is toxic. As war and capitalism feed each other, they throw fuel on each other's fire, acerbating each other's pointlessness. War nihilistically displaces society's ability to meet its needs. Society is no longer good to itself. It no longer makes infrastructure improvements. It no longer maintains humane safety nets such as Social Security, Medicare, and unemployment insurance. It no longer supports education and health care. It no longer regulates industry to protect the environment and the people who live in it. Consider Andrew J. Bacevich's observation in light of Durkheim's nightmare.

> At the end of the day, whether the United States is able to shape the Greater Middle East will matter less than whether it can reshape itself, restoring effectiveness to self-government, providing for sustainable and equitable prosperity, and extracting from a vastly diverse culture something to hold in common of greater moment than shallow digital enthusiasms and the worship of celebrity. Perpetuating the War for the Greater Middle East is not enhancing American freedom, abundance, and security. If anything, it is having the opposite effect. (2016, 370)

When war and capitalism work hand in hand, society neglects itself as a society, which is fatal.

Society is not simply a means to an end, say, to protect private property or promote free markets, as neoliberalism tells us. Society is an end-in-itself. Durkheim explains, "That such anarchy is an unhealthy phenomenon is quite evident, since it runs counter to the aim of society, which is to suppress, or at least to moderate, war among men, subordinating the law of the strongest to a higher law" (Durkheim 1933, 3). What is the law of the strongest? One way to formulate the law of the strongest is with the popular conviction that it is better to do wrong than suffer wrong. Because one is stronger, one is able to do wrong rather than suffer wrong. Such is the message in the video depicting the murder of George Floyd. The video is like a snuff film where the police officer, Derek Chauvin (while his police colleagues held Floyd down) sits on Floyd's neck for eight minutes and forty-six seconds while Floyd says sixteen times, "I can't breath" (O'Toole 2020, 25). Many in the United States watched the video which repeats the message that the law of the strongest governs the police force in their work and interactions with African Americans. In the police force there is an anti-black racism. At this point, society, which the police are sworn to protect, is invisible.

What is the higher law that suppresses or at least moderates the law of the strongest, that Durkheim only cryptically mentions? What is the aim of society? Let us turn to Plato. The higher law would be that it is better to suffer wrong than do wrong. This strange and counterintuitive argument is developed in Plato's *Gorgias*. We, of course, do not want to suffer wrong. We want to protect ourselves from suffering wrong. We, though, do not protect ourselves from suffering wrong by doing wrong. Doing wrong, in fact, leads to greater suffering, a suffering of the soul. Socrates argues that doing wrong leads to the greatest of all sufferings, which the police officer who killed Floyd, according to Socrates, is now experiencing. To protect ourselves from the greatest of all sufferings, we do all we can to avoid doing wrong. This higher law establishes a social order that is moral, one not based on force, and suppresses or at least moderates the law of the strongest. The protests across the nation against the endless murders of African Americans and other people of color by police officers seek to restore the higher law. The protests demand to restore society vis-á-vis the law of the strongest that the police officers grotesquely exemplified in the video. For Durkheim, the higher law is the raison d'etre of society.

There are other ways to formulate what Durkheim refers to as a higher law than the law of the strongest. In his critique of utilitarianism and the Hobbesian understanding of social order, Talcott Parsons articulates a higher law that serves the aim of society. "There would seem then to be not merely a separation of egoism and rationality . . . , but a reverse connection, with increasing rationality man becomes less rather than more egoistic" (1968, 162). Again, the logic is strange and counterintuitive. The logic behind the law of the strongest, of course, is that egoism and rationality are connected. Rationality serves ego's self-interest. Parsons, however, is articulating a higher law that supports society's aim. Altruism is more rational than ego-ism; egoism is less rational.

Like Marx and Durkheim, Weber was also afraid of capitalism. Weber's fear of capitalism is found in his account of charismatic legitimacy. Weber formulates three types of legitimate political domination. One type of politi-cal legitimacy is patriarchal or traditional authority. Another type of political legitimacy is bureaucratic or legal-rational authority. Another type of politi-cal legitimacy is charismatic authority. Each is an ideal type. There is no pure illustration of any of these three types in everyday or political life.

Weber connects and explains each type in relation to the economy. The responsibility of patriarchal power or traditional authority is to control those sections of the economy concerned with the supply of normal everyday re-quirements. The responsibility of bureaucracy is the same, "only expressed in more rational terms" (Weber 1978, 226). Bureaucracy uses a system of ra-tional rules and codes, efficient procedures for managing the economy. Char-ismatic authority contrasts with bureaucratic.

> In contrast with all forms of bureaucratic administrative systems, the charis-matic structure recognizes no forms or orderly procedures for appointment or dismissal, no "career," no "advancement," no "salary"; there is no organized training either for the bearer of charisma or his aides, no arrangements for supervision or appeal, no allocation of local areas of control or exclusive areas of competence, and finally no standing institutions comparable to bureaucratic "governing bodies" independent of persons and of their purely personal charis-ma. Rather, charisma recognizes only those stipulations and limitations which come from within itself. (Weber 1978, 227)

When an efficient, rational bureaucracy controls capitalism, capitalism may flourish for the benefit of society. Rational, effective bureaucratic leadership promises to sustain a stable and (perhaps) healthy capitalism. When charis-matic legitimacy controls capitalism, capitalism becomes demented and per-verse. Capitalism thrives on exchange-value over and above use-value, and the strength of exchange value is its charismatic character.

The charismatic legitimacy of President Donald Trump exemplifies We-ber's points on the spirit of capitalism. Often Trump's personality flaws are the focus for political pundits. Some focus on his rhetoric and its intense demagoguery with its dark consequences. Others address Trump's fascist attitudes. Few take up a more awkward question: what is it exactly that fuels Trump's legitimacy? What makes him a powerful US president?

Robert Reich (2016) makes an astute observation: President Trump's sup-porters support him precisely for the qualities he is criticized for, namely, his bigotry, megalomania, narcissism, xenophobia, and so on. The more rational pundits' criticism of Trump, the more this criticism empowers him. The more moral pundits' critique of Trump, the more it emboldens him. Here is the difficulty with the endless critiques of Trump's presidency in the *New York Times* and *Washington Post*.

To his supporters disenfranchised by the global economy and the condes-cending elite in Washington, Trump looks like a natural leader in a time of spiritual, economic, and ethical decay. Trump is the embodiment of the spirit of capitalism. He is not appointed, nor trained. He is neither a specialist nor a professional. He appears, simply appears, to possess a certain gift, a knack, that his supporters regard as supernatural, which is special because it is not available, as his fallen opponents demonstrate, to everyone.

Fox TV and radio shows with Rush Limbaugh thus empower Trump. To maintain the loyalty of his following, Trump must prove himself every day, and he can do so in whatever way imaginable. The more outrageous, the more spectacular, the more irrational, the more amoral, the better this is for strengthening his charismatic authority. Recommending disinfectants as a cure for the coronavirus is surreal and unintelligible, but it is real and intelli-gible from the viewpoint of the magical powers of the charismatic leader. The charismatic leader acquires the right to dominate by proving his powers in real life in whatever way he can, and these powers are seen as superior to science and reason.

Trump's charisma will fail to overcome the pandemic. He will fall, not because an opponent defeats him, but because the reality of the corona pan-demic defeats him. The pandemic exposes the nihilism and toxicity in Trump's charismatic legitimacy. Charisma thrives in a consequenceless world. Charisma sees itself as the only thing of consequence. The pandemic represents the consequential force of nature. Trump's followers do not see and do not accept what the light of the pandemic reveals as a necessary consequence of nature, which is a lamentable testimony to the powerfulness of Trump's charismatic legitimacy.

Charismatic authority mocks science. It silences bureaucratic authority, as witnessed by Trump's dismantling of the federal agencies that had the fore-sight to anticipate and plan for a pandemic. Trump insults Congress, the State Department, and the press. He weakens the World Health Organization cutting funding from the United States. The rationality and formal organization of these institutions (attributes needed to address the pandemic intelligently and humanely) are threats to Trump. Weber (1978, 230) explains where Trump is coming from.

> Genuinely charismatic justice is always rule-free in this sense: in its pure form it is completely opposed to all the bonds of formalism and tradition and is as free in its attitude to the sanctity of tradition as to rationalistic deductions from abstract concepts.

Trump's rule-free use of Twitter exemplifies Weber's point about charisma and explains why Trump takes angry exception to Twitter setting limits on his ability to glorify violence, engage in character assassinations, and promote falsehoods.

Weber's fear of capitalism is perhaps more prophetic than Marx or Durkheim's. Wall Street has done well under the charismatic leadership of Trump. Hillary Clinton's claim to rule had been grounded in her experience in government, her strong sense of bureaucratic authority. The people in the United States would not have found a better bureaucratic president. Clinton knew the system of practical rationality that structures the US government. The rules of the system are grounded not so much in something sacred or a traditional heritage but rather in their utilitarian calculability. People with bureaucratic authority are able to replace one set of rules with another set whenever it is rational to do so and whenever it better serves the country's or class's self-interest.

Trump, though, has served Wall Street better than Clinton would have. Under Trump the stock market has been profitable for the bourgeoise. The stock market serves as Trump's grateful bodyguard. Since Trump helps Wall Street unconditionally, Wall Street helps him unconditionally. The relationship is a master/slave relation. The paradox is that this charismatic rule of Wall Street rejects "as dishonorable all rational planning in the acquisition of money, and in general all rational forms of economy" (Weber 1978, 231). Trump unmasks the dynamic that was implicitly operating when President Obama resolved the foreclosure crises in 2010 with gargantuan government bailouts for the banks and leniency toward big-bank executives responsible for the crises. The solution at the same time forced millions of Americans out of their homes.

It will be a challenge for the government of the United States to switch from charismatic authority to bureaucratic authority, something the Democratic National Party and moderate Democrats, given their loyalty to Wall Street, do not adequately grasp. Leftist and socialist critiques of capitalism are direct. They assume the legitimacy of capitalism is surely in doubt, and they have compelling principles with which to make this assumption. These critiques, however, have remained largely inconsequential in the United States, as witnessed in the strong resistance to Bernie Sanders' presidential campaign. Sanders was a charismatic figure among young voters, but his campaign was based not on either charismatic or bureaucratic legitimacy but on traditional legitimacy. Sanders was committed to the political heritage reflected in the Civil Rights Movement that respects the human rights of all. This traditional authority within the context of American history is what Robert Bellah et al. (2007) in *Habits of the Heart* calls the Republican tradition, rooted in the value orientations grounded the best of American politics (Abraham Lincoln, Thomas Jefferson, Dr. Martin Luther King). The Democratic Party would do well to heed how the legitimacy which Sanders represents is superior not only to the charismatic legitimacy of Trump, but also to the bureaucratic legitimacy of the Clintons and Obamas. It is, after all, this same legitimacy that helped Obama win his election to the presidency in 2008.

Bureaucratic and charismatic leadership leave capitalism's hegemony unchallenged. Whether under charismatic or bureaucratic leadership, "The executive of the modern state is but a committee for managing the common affairs of the whole bourgeoisie" (Marx 1977, 38). The legitimacy of capitalism persists, and it is this phenomenon that Weber explains as the spirit of capitalism. Charisma sustains predatory capitalism. Charisma permits booty capitalism, where the government bails out banks and oil companies at the start of the coronavirus pandemic. These bailouts, when so many are destitute and unable to survive, supply the material needs of wealthy corporations, not for exchange or economic reasons, but simply to obtain material goods. Charismatic authority is an anti-economic force. Charisma allows gangster capitalism where the health care industry and pharmaceutical companies use the bank robber's line, "Your money or your life." Weber's analysis shows that it is necessary to unravel the two forms of authority that sustain today's capitalism, charismatic and bureaucratic.

> One can only understand the double nature of what one might call "the spirit of capitalism," and equally the specific features of the modern professionalized, bureaucratic form of everyday capitalism if one learns to make the conceptual distinction between these two structural elements, which are thoroughly entangled with one another, but are in the last analysis distinct. (Weber 1978, 231)

Capitalism threatens society as today's wars do. We would do well to understand the fear of capitalism that Marx, Durkheim, and Weber each articulated in particular ways. For Marx, capitalism was a tidal wave in the ocean of world history. For Durkheim, capitalism was a shattering earthquake at the epicenter of society. For Weber, capitalism, when ruled charismatically, was an insidious and invisible virus. The coronavirus pandemic now helps us see empirically what Marx, Durkheim, and Weber saw in a clear, theoretical way.

NOTE

This chapter was first presented at International Forum Bosnia, Sixth International Conference *Sarajevo and the World in Pandemic Perspectives*, Sarajevo, April–May 2020.

Chapter Nine

How an Apology Works

Exit from Sociocide

What repairs the wounds of sociocide? What restores the social? Consider the apology, which Lynndie England would not give to her enemy (Estes 2012), as a salve for healing the injury of sociocide.

An apology is an expression of regret. We say, I am sorry. When we apologize, we act. We address an audience. We act in the sense that the apology shows we are conscious of the other, the reality of the other, who is there before us. Why do we apologize? We apologize because we see the other. We identify with the other who we wronged. In doing so, we are required to apologize. An apology says that we now exist for another and we no longer exist exclusively for ourselves. An apology is not an attitude of abasement or humiliation before the other. It is an act of identifying with the other who we wronged.

A confession is different. A confession is an admission of guilt. A confession says morality is no longer something external to ourselves, to which we were only abstractly connected. A confession reveals that morality is something from which we can no longer live apart. A confession shows, perhaps only to God and ourselves, that we need morality to be ourselves. We renounce our self-centered self-existence. A confession exemplifies an inner, change in ourselves.

In Plato's *Republic*, to discern what justice truly is, Socrates said it would be easier to look at states rather than individuals. The subject of inquiry, justice, becomes bigger making it easier to see what we are trying to understand. Let us adopt this approach to try to understand the apology and the confession. We will look at apologies given by states rather than individuals.

It may be easier to discern what we are looking at by looking at examples of national apologies at the macro level.

In 2010, the British Prime Minister David Cameron offered an apology before the House of Commons for the 1972 "Bloody Sunday" killings of fourteen unarmed protesters in Northern Ireland (Fasternberg 2010). He said the British paratroopers' massacre of peacefully protesting Catholic protesters was "unjustified and unjustifiable." On another occasion, Cameron, however, chose not to give a British apology for the Amritsar massacre in India in 1919, in which at least 379 innocent people were killed. Cameron noted Winston Churchill had called the massacre a deeply shameful event when the massacre occurred. Churchill confesses to the shame of the Amritsar massacre. Since Churchill had made a confession, Cameron did not feel obliged to follow up with an apology. Can they exist separate from each other?

During the Holocaust commemoration of the Jewish victims in the Warsaw ghetto in Poland in 1970, the Chancellor of West Germany, Willy Brandt, dropped to his knees (Fasternberg 2010). He did not utter a word. He said he did what people do when words fail them carrying the burden of the millions who were murdered. When Brandt fell to his knees, *kniefall*, he confessed. He was genuinely contrite. He, though, did not say the words, "I am sorry" or utter an apology. It would be difficult to apologize for genocide, an unspeakable crime, a crime that stands outside of language. It would be hard for the victims of genocide to accept a verbal apology for what was inherently unspeakable. The verbal apology would be insulting. The verbal apology would fail to grasp the unspeakably egregious character of that for which it was apologizing. Presuming to speak what was inherently unspeakable replicates the crime.

In 2008, the US Congress apologized to African Americans for the racial injustices during the eras of slavery and Jim Crow (Fasternberg 2010). At the same time, the US Congress said its apology could not be used as a legal rationale for reparations. There was thus an apology but no confession. The US Congress refused to take responsibility for the consequences of the social injustices of racism and prejudice for which it was apologizing. If a confession had come, it would have exemplified a change of heart, a change in the self, and reparations would logically have followed. Did the US Congress understand the unspeakably egregious harm of racism in the United States?

With the signing of the Civil Liberties Act of 1988, President Ronald Reagan apologized to Japanese Americans during World War II who had been given ten days to sell their homes and businesses and were forced into internment camps (Fasternberg 2010). Two years later, President George W. Bush paid $20,000 in reparations to all surviving victims of the internment camps. The apology and the confession came together; they worked in tandem.

In 2007, Japan offered a formal apology to the 200,000 "comfort women" in Korea that the Japanese Imperial Army forced into sexual slavery during World War II when Japan established a network of "comfort stations" to which women were trafficked and used as sexual slaves. Japan pledged 1 billion yen ($8.3M) for the creation of a South Korean foundation to support with services the surviving South Korean victims. South Korea, in turn, pledged to drop its demand for reparation, end all criticism of Japan on the issue, and remove a memorial constructed by Korean "comfort women" survivors in 2011 in front of Japan's Embassy in Seoul, Korea (Fasternberg 2010).

Japan, however, did not mention or apologize to the many women who were victims of Japanese "comfort stations" in China, the Philippines, Timor-Leste, and other Asian countries during World War II. While Japan gave an apology to the women in Korea, it did not make a genuine confession. Political and instrumental reasons limit the scope and character of an apology. The dread of losing face and the shame of admitting to war crimes or worse, genocide, hinder making a confession.

In 2011, Cameron Munter, the US ambassador to Pakistan asked President Obama to apologize to Pakistan for the deaths of two dozen Pakistani soldiers killed in NATO airstrikes. An apology, the ambassador argued, would defuse the anger the people in Pakistan felt toward the United States. Following the advice of the Defense Department and military leaders, President Obama declined to make an apology. Secretary of State Hillary Clinton instead offered expressions of remorse. If President Obama were to go against the advice of the Defense Department, it would have been fodder for his Republican opponents. Note, however, that "A man should never be ashamed to own he has been in the wrong, which is but saying, in other words, that he is wiser today than he was yesterday." When Secretary of State Clinton offered expressions of remorse, she is giving neither an apology nor a confession. There is no recognition of the other. There is no change in the self. Expressions of remorse are a face-saving gesture.

In 2012, the president of Serbia, Tomislav Nikolić apologized on behalf of Serbia for the 1995 massacre of 8,000 Muslims in the Bosnian town of Srebrenica. When Nikolić said, "I am down on my knees because of it. Here, I am down on my knees. And I am asking for a pardon for Serbia for the crime that was committed in Srebrenica. I apologise for the crimes committed by any individual on behalf of our state and our people," he evokes the image of Brandt's *kniefall* at the Holocaust commemoration in Poland without, however, having such an action observed in public. In 2004, the United Nations war crimes court had ruled that the 1995 Srebrenica massacre was genocide. In 2012, Nikolić, however, declined to characterize the killings as an act of genocide.When asked by a reporter to agree that all the evidence showed that Srebrenica had suffered a genocide, Nikolić said the charge remained to be proven. Nikolić refused to confess to genocide; nor would he apologize for genocide, actions which could have led to reconciliation and peace in the Balkans.

The apology without a confession and the confession without an apology exemplify hypocrisy. However contrite Brandt's confession is, without the apology (no matter how impossibe to give), it may seem unconvincing to the victims of genocide. However genuine the apology of the US Congress to African Americans, without the confession, the apology seems self-serving. Each is one-sided. Each hides a latent contempt for morality, playing on the conditionality of moral principle and offering at best a dissemblance of moral principle. The function of the hypocrisy is to maintain the desired freedom of opposing what is moral and heeding one's own inner law (Hegel 1977, 370–395). The function of the hypocrisy is to keep for oneself a law of individuality and caprice, putting the nonmoral consciousness before the moral consciousness. The function is to sustain the belief that, in fact, it is better to do wrong than suffer wrong. As long as the primacy of the nonmoral consciousness is maintained, forgiveness is impossible as a reciprocal understanding. The other who is wronged has not been genuinely recognized. The self of the one who committed injustice has made no change in the self that committed the wrong.

When a confession exemplifies an inner change of the self that affirms an essential relation to what is moral and when an apology genuinely recognizes the other and the other's reality, forgiveness becomes real. Here is where individuals have an advantage over states. It is easier for individuals to apologize and confess, keeping the two sisters together. As Hegel (1977, 676) in the section titled "Evil and the Forgiveness of It" puts it: "Breaking the hard heart and raising it to the level of universality is the same process which was expressed in the case of the consciousness that openly made its confession. The wounds of the spirit heal and leave no scars behind."

The apology and confession need to be based on good will. What then is good will? Aristotle writes:

> It would surely be ridiculous to wish for the good of wine: if one wishes it at all, it is that the wine may keep, so that we can have it for ourselves. But men say that we ought to wish for the good of our friend for the friend's sake. When people wish for our good in this way, we attribute good will toward them, if the same wish is not reciprocated by us. (1962, 217–218).

It is ridiculous, Aristotle says, to wish for the good of wine. We wish for the good of wine, Aristotle notes, with respect to our advantage, that it may taste good or may keep. We do not, he says, wish for the good of wine with respect to wine per se. Aristotle points out two important features of good will. First, good will is wishing for the good of the other for the sake of the other. Second, the appropriate context for good will is a human relationship.

Good will is not dependent upon its effects, for example, its being reciprocated. The expectation that good will should be returned belies the character of good will. Good will is independent of cause and effect explanations as a viable epistemology for human understanding. Good will is autonomous; it is an expression of the free will of the human being toward another human being. A confession and an apology need to be given freely to be genuine. The significance of its autonomy is that it is neither dependent upon nor controlled by whatever events it may or may not affect.

Jürgen Habermas says, "From the beginning philosophy has presumed that the autonomy and responsibility posited with the structure of language are not only anticipated but real" (1971, p. 314). Recall Socrates' argument that human beings never knowingly do wrong. Socrates cannot imagine someone doing something wrong, unjust, or evil and knowing, truly knowing, that what he or she did was wrong, unjust, or evil. When a person murders, he or she does not really know, despite his or her awareness of the normative order, that what he or she does is wrong. If the murderer had in fact known that it is wrong to murder, he or she would not have so acted. Habermas states a Socratic conviction: "The autonomy and responsibility posited with the structure of language are not only anticipated but real" (1971, 314).

For Habermas and Socrates, good will does not mean that we ingenuously endow the other with a good heart but that, in knowing the other, we are subject to the principle of good will even in its apparent absence. Habermas and Socrates are not making an empirical point; rather, they are showing good will toward humanity as a way to begin as well as govern their inquiry into the nature of humanity.

In the Republic we read:

> Now, Thrasymachus did not agree to all of this so easily as I tell it now, but he dragged his feet and resisted, and he produced a wonderful quantity of sweat, for it was summer. And then I saw what I had not yet seen before—Thrasymachus blushing. (1968, 29)

Although there are several good commentaries on this exchange between Thrasymachus and Socrates, none ever mention or comment on Thrasymachus's blushing. Jacob Klein argues that the Platonic dialogue is a literary text and so must be addressed as such—"What is being said in a Platonic dialogue must be watched most carefully: every word [verbal and nonverbal] counts; some casually spoken words [or nonverbal communication] may be more important than lengthy, elaborate statements" (1977, 2). Let us follow Klein's advice. Why does Thrasymachus, once he sees that he is refuted regarding his argument that injustice is better than justice, blush? Why does Thrasymachus not, like Anytus in Plato's *Meno*, get angry, admonish Socrates, and walk away? Why does Thrasymachus not, like Callicles in the *Gorgias*, simply refuse to answer any more of Socrates' questions? Thrasymachus's blush is an expression of his experience upon being refuted. While certainly involuntary (one cannot blush at will), the blush still comes from within Thrasymachus: It reveals his inner nature.

The blush exemplifies the will of Thrasymachus as he realizes that he is caught within a significant contradiction. The blush reveals Thrasymachus's awareness of the contradiction between what he was arguing for, i.e., that the unjust are stronger and so better than the just, and what he knows. Thrasymachus's argument that injustice is superior to justice lacks power, and this makes him blush. When Thrasymachus argues for injustice, his will is at odds with itself. Socrates (Plato 1968, 29) himself is taken aback when he sees Thrasymachus blush, "And then I saw what I had not seen before."

Habermas says, "The truth of statements is based on anticipating the realization of the good life" (1971, 314). Habermas captures the integrity of good will. Some social theorists desire neither to exemplify nor to sustain the principle of good will as what guides human inquiry. Some oppose the idea. One example is Michel Foucault, who indicates that the idea of good will is really the weakest and perhaps least significant human interest with respect to human understanding in social discourse. Foucault resists the principle of good will, because to him it represents the denial and repression of other more "real" human interests—interests in power, pleasure, survival, self-satisfaction, and so on. Foucault's theorizing does not acknowledge a need within theoretical inquiry to distinguish the way in which we orient to a concrete other, i.e., that other who exemplifies soullessness, e.g., wine, and the way in which we orient to a human other, i.e., that other who exemplifies soul. For Foucault, the distinction is immaterial and in and of itself perverse for grasping the true, positivistic reality of human nature. Speaking to the character of his theoretical work, Foucault says:

> . . . criticism is no longer going to be practiced in the search for formal structures with universal value, . . . criticism is not transcendental, and its goal is not that of making a metaphysics possible . . . it will not seek to identify the universal structures of all knowledge or of all possible moral action . . . it will not deduce from the form of what we are what is impossible for us to do and to know. . . . It is not seeking to make possible a metaphysics that has finally become a science, it is seeking to give new impetus to the undefined work of freedom. (1987, 170)

What does Foucault's theorizing do? It seeks to give new impetus to the "undefined work of freedom." Foucault does not want to be coerced by the authority of metaphysics, e.g., which Plato would refer to as truth, beauty, or justice. With the term "the undefined work of freedom," Foucault reformulates autonomy as autocratic, that freedom that is "undefined," therefore unlimited, and not itself subject to responsibility. The concept of good will discloses a commitment to "the search for formal structures with universal value" (1987, 170), which Foucault says it is impossible for us ever to possess. As Thrasymachus' blush, however, shows, it is equally impossible for us to divorce ourselves from "formal structures with universal value." Such is our fate as human beings, and good will keeps us in touch with this fate.

Can this be? Can society be killed? Is there an immortal character to society? Is society based upon nonempirical phenomena more than empirical sociology might care to admit? The possibility of the social is never erased entirely. The gift of mental integrity is never impossible to exemplify. Let us draw to a close with a story from a war zone observed and recently remembered during the pandemic by the journalist, Barbara Demick (2020).

> The Bosnian war was largely an ethnic conflict, started by Serb nationalists who objected to Bosnia's secession from what remained of Yugoslavia and so took to the mountains surrounding the city, cutting it off from the outside world. But many moderate Serbs supported the new Bosnian government and remained in Sarajevo, under constant bombardment from their nationalist brethren. On the street where I was living, the mostly Muslim residents went out of their way to be kind to the remaining Serbs. The neighbors used to bring food to an elderly widow, even though her son had joined the Serb militias bombing the city from the mountains. What surprised me most was that my landlords (we were one of the few houses with a working telephone) would allow this son, an enemy soldier, to call her phone to speak to his mother. Whenever he rang, no matter how late, the landlady would run out to fetch the Serb widow to talk to her son, then send her home with a gift of bread or vegetables. It was not necessarily that these Sarajevans had superhuman qualities of compassion and there were many who were not so tolerant. But people recognized that their goal was not merely to outlive the siege, but to preserve their civilization. To survive the siege, they had to constantly remind themselves who they were in the past and what they hoped to be in the future.

The siege of Sarajevo was brutal; its pathos and wretchedness have been repeated in war after war, whether it be in Afghanistan, Iraq, Syria, Libya, Yemen, or elsewhere where wars today are taking place. The good will toward the Serb widow whose son was an enemy soldier was not exactly friendship. It was simply good will. Good will cannot be quantified, nor operationalized. Parsons (1968, 424) says, "Action is not only 'meaningfully oriented,' as the positivist inevitably concludes, to reality as rationally understood by science but to the nonempirical as well." Good will is meaningfully oriented to the nonempirical. Good will preserves the social no matter how unconscionable the violence the social suffers. When society does not exist, that is, when the nonempirical elements have evaporated, nihilism exists. When society exists, when nonempirical elements exist, nihilism evaporates.

Bibliography

Agamben, Giorgio. 2000. *Means without Ends: Notes on Politics*. Translated by Vincenzo and Cesare Casarino. Minneapolis, MN: University of Minnesota Press.

Alleg, Henri. 2006. *The Question*. Lincoln: University of Nebraska.

Andrić, Ivo. 1977. *The Bridge on the Drina*. Translated by Lovett F. Edwards. Chicago: University of Chicago Press.

Anzulovic, Branimir. 1999. *Heavenly Serbia: From Myth to Genocide*. New York: New York University Press.

Arendt, Hannah. 1944. "The Jew as Pariah: A Hidden Tradition." *Jewish Social Studies* 6 (2): 99–122.

Aristotle. 1962. *Nicomachean Ethics*. Translated by Martin Ostwald. Indianapolis: Bobbs-Merrill.

Bacevich, Andrew J. 2016. *America's War for the Greater Middle East: A Military History*. New York: Random House.

Banac, Ivo. 1993. "Separating History from Myth: An Interview with Ivo Banac." In *Why Bosnia?*, edited by R. Ali and L. Lifschultz, 134–165. Stony Creek, CT: Pamphleteer's Press.

Banerjee, Abhijit V., and Duflo, Ester. 2019. *Good Economic for Hard Times*. New Delhi: Juggernaut Books.

Bellah, Robert N. et al. 2007. *Habits of the Heart: Individualism and Commitment in American Life*. Berkeley: University of California Press.

Blasim, Hussan. 2014. *The Corpse Exhibition and Other Stories of Iraq*. Translated by Jonathan Wright. New York: Penguin Books.

Blum, Alan. 1992. "Victim, Patient, Client, Pariah: Steps in the Self-Understanding of Suffering and Affliction." *Canadian Journal of Visual Impairment* 1:64–82.

Broz, Svetlana. 2004. *Good People in an Evil Time: Portraits of Complicity and Resistance in the Bosnian War*. Translated by Ellen Elias-Bursać. New York: Other Press.

Buber, Martin. 1958. *I and Thou*. Translated by Ronald Gregor Smith. New York: Macmillan, 1958.

Bruce, Andrea. 2008. "Grim Ritual at the Baghdad Morgue." *The Washington Post*, October 26, 2008. http://voices.washingtonpost.com/unseen-iraq/2008/10/unseen_iraq_1027.html.

Burke, Kenneth. 1969. *A Grammar of Motives*. Berkeley: University of California Press.

Butler, Thomas. 2001. "The Hagueing of Slobodan Milošević and the Struggle for the Soul of Serbia." Unpublished manuscript (cited with author's permission).

Christie, Debbie. 1992. *War: We Are All Neighbors* [Video documentary]. London: Granada Television.

Danner, Mark. 2006. "Iraq: The War of the Imagination." *The New York Review of Books* 53 (3). December 21, 2006.
Demick, Barbara. 2020. "Op-Ed: How Living Through the Siege of Sarajevo Prepared Me for Coronavirus." *Los Angeles Times*, April 7, 2020.
Dicosola, Maria. 2016. "Ethnic Federalism and Political Rights of the Others in Bosnia and Herzegovina." In *Proceedings of the Conference Twenty Years after Dayton. The Constitutional Transition of Bosnia and Herzegovina*, edited by Ludovica Benedizione and Valentina Rita Scotti, 134–165. Rome: Luiss University Press.
Đorđević, Mirko. 1996. "Serbia's Ark in the Eye of the Storm." *War Report* 40:28–30.
Doubt, Keith, and Tufekčić, Adnan. 2019. *Ethnic and National Identity in Bosnia-Herzegovina: Kinship and Solidarity in a Polyethnic Society*. Lanham: Lexington Books.
Doubt, Keith. 2014. *Through the Window: Kinship and Elopement in Bosnia-Herzegovina*. Budapest: Central European University Press.
Dower, John W. 2010. *Cultures of War: Pearl Harbor / Hiroshima / 9-11 / Iraq*. New York: W. W. Norton.
Duby, Georges. 2007. *Love and Marriage in the Middle Ages*. Chicago: University of Chicago.
DuBois, W. E. B. 2016. *The Souls of Black Folks*. New York: Dover Publications.
Durkheim, Émile. 2003. "On Mechanical and Organic Solidarity." In *Social Theory: Roots and Branches*, edited by P. Kivisto, 38–42. Los Angeles, CA: Roxbury Publishing.
Durkheim, Émile. 1975. *Durkheim on Religion*, edited by W. S. F. Pickering. New York: Oxford University Press.
Durkheim, Émile. 1973. "Individualism and the Intellectuals." In *On Morality and Society*, edited by Robert Bellah, 43–58. Chicago: University of Chicago Press.
Durkheim, Émile. 1933. *The Division of Labor in Society in Society*. New York: Macmillan.
Durkheim, Émile. 1915. *The Elementary Forms of Religious Life*. Translated by George Ward G. Swain. London: George & Unwin.
Dworkin, Ronald. 2013. *Justice for Hedgehogs*. Cambridge: Belknap Press.
Dworkin, Ronald. 1977. *Taking Rights Seriously*. Cambridge, MA: Harvard University Press.
Edelstein, David. 2006. "Now Playing at Your Local Multiplex: Torture Porn." *New York*, January 26, 2006.
Edwards, David, and Nick Juliano. 2007. "Iraqi Volunteers Bury More Anonymous Victims of Violence Now Than During Saddam's Rule: CNN." CNN's Newsroom, September 14, 2007.
Eisenhower, Dwight D. 1961. "Farewell Address by President Dwight D. Eisenhower." January 17, 1961; Final TV Talk 1/17/61 (1), Box 38, Speech Series, Papers of Dwight D. Eisenhower as President, 1953–1961, Eisenhower Library. National Archives and Records Administration.
Estes, Adam Clark. 2012. "Eight Years after Abu Ghraib, Lynndie England's Not Doing So Well." *The Atlantic*, March 19, 2012.
Fanon, Fanz. 1968. *The Wretched of the Earth*. Translated by Constance Farrington. New York: Grove Press.
Fasternberg, Dan. 2010. "Top 10 National Apologies," *Time*, June 17, 2010. http://content.time.com/time/specials/packages/article.
Fassihi, Farnaz. 2008. *Waiting for an Ordinary Day: The Unraveling of Life in Iraq*. New York: Public Affairs.
Filkins, Dexter. 2009. *The Forever War*. New York: Vintage Books.
Foucault, Michel. 1987. "What Is Enlightenment?" In P. Rabinow and W. M. Sullivan (Eds.), *Interpretive Social Science: A Second Look*, edited Paul Rabinow and William M. Sullivan, 157–174. Berkeley: University of California Press.
Foucault, Michel. 1978. *The History of Sexualities: Volume 1, An Introduction*. New York: Pantheon.
Freud, Sigmund. 1949. *An Outline of Psycho-Analysis*. New York: W. W. Norton & Company.
Galtung, Johan. 1982. *Environment, Development, and Military Activity: Towards Alternative Security Doctrines*. New York: Columbia University Press.
Girard, René. 1977. *Violence and the Sacred*. Baltimore, MD: John Hopkins University Press.
Habermas, Jürgen. 1971. *Knowledge and Human Interest*. Boston: Beacon Press.

Hatzfeld, Jean. 2009. *The Antelope's Strategy: Living in Rwanda after the Genocide.* New York: Farrar, Straus and Giroux.

Hayden, Robert M. 1995. "Focus: Constitutionalism and Nationalism in the Balkans." *East European Constitutional Review* 5 (fall): 68–75.

Hegel, G. W. F. 1977. *The Phenomenology of Mind.* Translated by J. B. Baillie. New York: Humanities Press.

Herlihy, D. 2004. "The Making of the Medieval Family: Symmetry, Structure, and Sentiment." In *Medieval Families: Perspectives on Marriage, Household, and Children*, edited by Carol Neel, 192–213. Toronto: University of Toronto Press.

Hobbes, Thomas. 1968. *Leviathan*, edited by by C. B. Macpherson. Middlesex, England: Penguin.

Horne, Alistair. 2006. *A Savage War of Peace: Algeria 1954–1962.* New York: NYRB Classics.

Jaspers, Karl. 2001. *The Question of German Guilt.* New York: Fordham University Press.

Kapić, Suada. 2000. *The Siege of Sarajevo: 1992–1996.* Ljubljana: FAMA Associates.

Kant, Immanuel. 1917. *Perpetual Peace: A Philosophical Essay.* London: George Allen and Unwin, 1917.

Kis, Janos, and Adam Michnik. 2008. "After Five Years." *The New York Review of Books*, July 17, 2008.

Klein, Jacob. 1977. *Plato's Trilogy: Theaetetus, the Sophist and the Statesman.* Chicago: University of Chicago Press.

Kluckhohn, Richard. 1964. *Culture and Behavior.* Glencoe: Free Press.

Kovač, Nikola. 2007. "Political Reflection." *Spirit of Bosnia/Duh Bosne* 2 (April). Retrieved at http://www.spiritofbosnia.org/volume-2-no-2-2007-april/political-reflection/.

Kroeber, A. L. 1923. *Anthropology.* New York: Harcourt, Brace, and Company.

Lievan, Anatol. 2012. *America Right or Wrong: An Anatomy of American Nationalism.* Oxford: University of Oxford Press.

Levin, Michael. 1982. "The Case for Torture," *Newsweek.* June 7, 1982.

Lorde, Audre. 1984. "The Tools of the Master Will Never Dismantle the Master's House." In *Sister Outsider: Essays and Speeches*, 100–103. Berkley: Crossing Press Feminist Series.

Luizard, Pierre-Jean. 2008. "Why the Pentagon Failed." *Le Novel Observateur*, March 20, 2008.

Lukić, Lidija. 2001. "Svetosavlje as Enlightened Nationalism." *Liberty.* Retrieved Oct. 26, 2005. http://www.snd-us.com/Liberty/lukic_svetosavlje.htm.

Magas, Branka. 1993. *The Destruction of Yugoslavia: Tracking the Break-Up, 1980–1992.* London: Verso.

Mahmutćehajuć, Rusmir. 2003. *Sarajevo Essays: Politics, Ideology, and Tradition.* Albany: State University Of New York.

Malinowski, Bronislaw. 1954. *Magic, Science, and Religion.* New York: Doubleday Anchor Books.

Mandel, Emily St. John. 2014. *Station Eleven.* New York: Vintage Books.

Marshall, Ingeborg. 1996. *A History and Ethnography of the Beothuk.* Montreal: McGill-Queen's University Press.

Marx, Karl. 2004. "Estranged Labor." In *Social Theory: The Multicultural and Classic Readings*, edited by Charles Lemert, 30–36. Boulder, CO: Westview.

Marx, Karl. 1977. *Manifesto of the Communist Party.* Moscow: Progress Publishers.

McCarthy, Cormac. 2006. *The Road.* New York: Vintage Books.

McKim, Richard. 1988. "Truth and Shame in Plato's *Gorgias.*" In *Platonic Writings/Platonic Readings*, edited by Charles L. Griswold, 34–48. University Park, PA: The Pennsylvania State University Press.

Mead, George Herbert. 1956. *On Social Psychology: Selected Papers*, edited by Anselm Strauss. Chicago: University of Chicago Press.

Mujkić, Asim. 2007. *We, the Citizens of Ethnopolis.* Sarajevo: Centar za ljudska prava Univerziteta u Sarajevo.

O'Toole, Fintan. 2020. "Unpresidented." *The New York Review of Books.* July 23, LXVII (12): 25–27.

Otterman, Michael, and Hil, Richard. 2010. *Erasing Iraq: The Human Costs of Carnage.* London: Pluto Press.

Palermo, Francesco. 2016. "Fish Soups, Chickens and Eggs, Mirrors and Miniatures: The Bosnian Question Two Decades after Dayton. Concluding Remarks." In *Proceedings of the Conference Twenty years after Dayton. The Constitutional Transition of Bosnia and Herzegovina,* edited by Ludovica Benedizione and Valentina Rita Scotti, 157–162. Rome: Luiss University Press.

Parsons, Talcott. 1968. *The Structure of Social Action: A Study in Social Theory with Special Reference to a Group of Recent European Writers.* New York: Free Press.

Paskaljević, Goran. 2011. *Optimisti.* Berlin: Nova Film, Zepter International, Swiss Effects, Wanda Visión, and Zillion Film.

Plato. *Gorgias.* 1971. Translated by Walter Hamilton. Middlesex, England: Penguin.

Plato. 1968. *The Republic of Plato.* Translated by Allan Bloom. New York: Basic Books.

Reich, Robert. 2016. "Why Trump Might Win." Webpage post, Robert Reich. https://robertreich.org/post/144763032115.

Rowley, Colleen, and McGovern, Ray. 2008. "Deterring Torture through the Law." Information Clearing House. http://www.informationclearinghouse.info/article21509.html.

Sartre, Jean-Paul. 2006. "Victory." In *The Question* by Henri Alleg, xxvii–xxxvi. Lincoln: University of Nebraska.

Saramago, José. 1997. *Blindness.* Orlando, FL: Harcourt, Inc.

Schwartz, Michael. 2008. *War without End: The Iraq War in Context.* Chicago: Haymarket Books.

Schell, Jonathan. 1982. *The Fate of the Earth.* New York: Knopf.

Secor, Laura. 1999. "Testaments Betrayed: Yugoslavian Intellectuals and the Road to War." *Lingua Franca* 9 (September), 1999. http://www.linguafranca.com/9909/testbet.html (accessed December 15, 2000; site now discontinued).

Semple, Kirk. 2006. "Relentless Sectarian Violence in Baghdad Stalks Its Victims Even at the Morgue." *New York Times,* July 30, 2006.

Shanker, Thom, and Bumiller, Elisabeth. 2011. "Looking Back, Gates Says He's Grown Wary of 'Wars of Choice.'" *New York Times,* June 18.

Sher, Gerson S. 1977. *Praxis: Marxist Criticism and Dissent in Socialist Yugoslavia.* Bloomington: Indiana University Press.

Sherman, Nancy. 2015. *Afterwar: Healing the Moral Wounds of Our Soldiers.* New York: Oxford University Press.

Silber, Laura, and Alan Little. 1996. *Yugoslavia: Death of a Nation.* New York: TV Books.

Skocpol, Theda. 1979. *States and Social Revolutions: A Comparative Analysis of France, Russia, and China.* Cambridge: Cambridge University Press.

Solecki, Ralph. 1971. *Shanidar: The First Flower People.* New York: Knopf.

Tavernise, Sabrina. 2005. "End of the Line for Families of Baghdad's Missing: The City Morgue." *New York Times,* May 20, 2005.

Tishkov, Valery. 2005. "Dynamics of a Society at War: Ethnographical Aspects." In *Chechnya: From Past to Future,* edited by Richard Sakwa, 157–180. London: Anthem Press.

Wagner, Sarah. 2008. *To Know Where He Lies: DNA Technology and the Search for Srebrenica's Missing.* Berkeley: University of California Press.

Weber Max. 1978. "The Nature of Charismatic Domination." In *Max Weber: Selections in Transition,* edited and translated by W. G. Runciman, 226–251. Cambridge: Cambridge University Press.

Weber, Max. 1947. *The Theory of Social and Economic Organization,* edited with an introduction by Talcott Parsons. New York: Oxford University Press.

Woodhead, Leslie. 1999. *A Cry from the Grave* [Video Documentary]. New York: Thirteen/WNET.

Žbanić, Jasmila. 2006. *Grbavica.* Sarajevo: Deblokada and COOP99.

Žižek, Slavoj. 2008. *Violence.* New York: Picador.

Index

About the Author

Keith Doubt holds his master's and doctorate degrees from York University, Toronto, Canada, where he studied with Peter McHugh and Alan Blum. He has published articles on a range of sociological theorists: Harold Garfinkel, Georg Simmel, Hans-Georg Gadamer, George Herbert Mead, Jürgen Habermas, Talcott Parsons, Erving Goffman, and Kenneth Burke. He is the author of *Towards a Sociology of Schizophrenia: Humanistic Reflections* (University of Toronto Press), *Sociology after Bosnia and Kosovo: Recovering Justice* (Rowman & Littlefield), *Sociologija nakon Bosne* (Buybook, Sarajevo), *Understanding Evil: Lessons from Bosnia* (Fordham University Press), *Through the Window: Kinship and Elopement in Bosnia-Herzegovina* (Central European University Press), and with Adnan Tufekčić *Ethnic and National Identity in Bosnia-Herzegovina: Kinship and Solidarity in a Polyethnic Society* (Lexington Books).

He was a Senior Fulbright Scholar in the Faculty of Political Science at University of Sarajevo in 2001 and held the Fulbright Distinguished Chair in the Department of Sociology at University of Innsbruck, Austria, in 2007. He was recipient of the Fulbright Flex Grant, involving both teaching and research in Tuzla, Bosnia-Herzegovina, in 2017, 2018, and 2019. At Wittenberg University he is professor emeritus. He is the founder and editor of the interdisciplinary, bilingual online journal, *Spirit of Bosnia/Duh Bosne*.

www.ingramcontent.com/pod-product-compliance
Lightning Source LLC
Chambersburg PA
CBHW022328280326
41932CB00010B/1266